YES,
GOD!

YES, GOD!

THE COST. THE SACRIFICE. THE BLESSINGS.

MICHELE NOEL-PEAKE

purposely
created
PUBLISHING

YES, GOD!
Published by Purposely Created Publishing Group™
Copyright © 2021 Michele Noel-Peake
All rights reserved.

Printed in the United States of America
ISBN: 978-1-64484-297-3

Special discounts are available on bulk quantity purchases by book clubs, associations and special interest groups. For details email: sales@publishyourgift.com or call (888) 949-6228.
For information log on to www.PublishYourGift.com

DEDICATION

This book is dedicated to Jesus Christ, my friend and Lord and Savior, to whom I am truly grateful for providing me with so many opportunities to say "yes, God."

I thank my two inspirations, my beautiful daughters, Zarina and Nia, who are just starting their incredible journey of saying "yes, God" for themselves.

A special dedication to my mom and dad, Evelyn and Berkley Noel, for training my brother and me up in the way that we should go.

And finally, I thank my husband and all of the people God has brought into my life as a result of saying "yes, God." You have been and continue to be a true blessing to me!

TABLE OF CONTENTS

FOREWORD

We are trusting God that the content of this book will inspire you to become more intimate with Jesus Christ, move you to daily seek your assignments, and encourage you to strive to glorify God.

In Isaiah 6, Isaiah was in service to the Lord, but not completely dedicated to Him. But the scriptures teach us that after his spiritual encounter with the Lord, he experienced a breakthrough. Yes . . . Isaiah came out of his box. God showed him a true reflection of himself as He aligned Isaiah alongside of Him. When we have a true experience with God, it is life-changing. We are no longer just working for God; rather, He is now working *in* us.

In order to have a substantial relationship with the Lord, we must admit to seeing what God sees in us. After seeing the vision, Isaiah said, "Woe is me, for I am undone! Because I am a man of unclean lips, . . . for my eyes have seen the King, the Lord of hosts" (Isaiah 6:5, NKJV). When we admit, believe, and confess, God releases saving grace and transforming power in our inner spirits. This is when our faith becomes genuine. At this point, we no longer need others to define the essence of who we are, nor do we need others to define the reality of Jesus Christ.

After Isaiah's spiritual encounter, he was able to hear and understand the voice of God. God gave a general call: "Who will take My message to Judah; whom shall I send?" Because of Isaiah's personal experiences, he declared, "Hear I am; send me, Lord, I will go." Get ready; be prepared to go, preach, and serve, even if you do not get the chance to activate your decision. Get ready!

I pray that as you read this book, you will experience more of God. If you have not received Him as your Savior, this will be your first encounter. It is our salvation that needs to become our lifestyle. For those who are already Christians, I pray that you will be inspired to allow God to open or reopen doors of opportunities and that you will grow. May the Spirit of Christ speak to you as you read this book.

Blessings,
Pastor Charles E. Cato, Sr.

PREFACE

Yes, God! was written to spread the powerful message that a "yes, God" is not only life-changing, but also necessary for true victory and success in our lives. Each coauthor in this book has experienced the power in saying yes to God, and each feels called by God to help as many people as possible experience the supernatural, life-changing power that comes with saying "yes, God."

I told God yes many years ago, and it has been the most painful and powerful thing I have ever consciously done in my life. You would think saying "yes, God" would make everything right with the world. Or so I thought at the time. What I didn't know, but slowly began to discover, is that saying "yes, God" would be the experience of a lifetime! I would experience things and people in supernatural ways! How exciting, exhilarating, terrifying, and crazy all at the same time! Here are seven individuals sharing not just their stories, but also some of the things they did, said, prayed, surrendered, and sacrificed in hopes that you too might implement some or all into your life.

This is why *Yes, God!* had to be written: so people everywhere could see, through the stories on these pages, that saying "yes, God" is a life-changer. It changes the entire game of your life. The stories on these pages are of real people who struggled and stretched and persevered beyond what they ever could have imagined was possible, not because they were worthy, but because they surrendered and said "yes, God"—and now they are walking in the victory of their "yes, God" moments.

Regardless of your struggle—whether you are feeling stressed and anxious about the times we are living in, grieving, or facing financial struggles, family challenges, or issues with sin—be encouraged by these stories. We want God's mercy, grace, and favor to be upon your life, and we pray that you are blessed beyond measure as you read through each powerful chapter in this book. May your faith increase by what you hear. May your strength increase in Him, and may your walk with Jesus be like never before!

Finally, my beautiful friends, we truly pray that you are *motivated* to seek God's will for your life. We pray that you are *inspired* to see more of what God has for you. And finally, we pray that you are *compelled* to say "yes, God" over and over again!

With much love,
Michele Noel-Peake

Go Deeper: You Have Nothing to Lose but Your Chains

Ashley McNeill

When I sit back and ask myself what the moment was when I committed and said, "Yes, God, I surrender," I can recall very clearly two things: 1) the incident and 2) the end result, my coming-to-Jesus moment. Interestingly, that's all I remember.

Some may call it weird—but I believe that God intentionally reminded me exactly what I needed to know to share this testimony with you all today. Let's get one thing straight—I haven't always been a Jesus-loving, Bible-thumping Christian. I've always loved God, don't get me wrong. I was born and raised in a Christian environment, from Baptist churches to Catholic school. However, it wasn't until I got serious about my faith in 2017 that I started to develop a deep love for Christ as well.

You may not understand, but that's okay. My goal is to express that the true process of spiritual breakthrough and elevation requires something different, something opposite of the mediocrity of before. I can confidently say from my experiences that the majority of us as Christians are mediocre when it comes to the things of Christ. It wasn't until my breaking point that I realized saying "I'm just a Christian" just won't suffice.

For the record, I wasn't desperately seeking God, nor was I searching for God at all. Rather, once I endured the deepest, darkest moments of my life, that *light* came on which changed my life forever. Let me explain . . .

THE PIT

One of the major factors that led to my pit experience was becoming a motherly confidant to my friends and family, who heavily relied on me daily for advice and solutions to their crises. In addition, I was struggling with my perspective of my own life after returning from a developing nation, having experienced their deprivation of basic human rights like clean water. Everything combined together, creating this voice in the back of my head that said, "You have no reason to be ungrateful. You have everything you could possibly need. Your problems are not real problems."

This was my life, on top of taking six classes, serving on the executive boards of three different clubs, and having a boyfriend that lived below the poverty line and struggled to meet daily necessities. Oh, and did I mention that he lived continents away, making it difficult to communicate? When I look back on all of this, I can see that my pit was caused by something simple . . . my reliance on others, including on a close relationship that turned out to be toxic. Now that I think about it, the pit was inevitable.

The crazy thing about pits is that you usually don't know you're in one until you're out of it. Even worse is when the pit you're in is like being in a state of darkness, surrounded by inescapable blackness. In my case, sin was my darkness, and I was surrounded by inescapable sin. It was as if I bought the 4-for-4 deal from Wendy's: I dabbled with four sins, and four came along for free. One "small" sin here, another "small" sin there; gradually, these "small" sins became justified to me, time and time again. At first, it was a game that I was dabbling in. Then, at some point, it was no longer a game . . . it had become an entire lifestyle of sin that I was thriving in. This was my story in a nutshell: the story of how a seemingly successful twenty-one year old was actually physically, spiritually, and emotionally deteriorating from the inside out.

In the eyes of my friends and family, I was a success story. I had just graduated, a first-gen college student. I had the world at my fingertips, with endless possibilities of what I could do, discover, and explore. My physical accolades were enough to keep them blinded and distracted from what was killing me internally. According to them, *she has the perfect life—no bills, no baby, no problems. She just graduated, she's travelling the world, and she's smart and beautiful. What could possibly be wrong with her?*

They didn't notice that in reality, I was an adult fully dressed in lust, drowning in a toxic relationship. I was an irresponsible and sometimes violent drinker that was secretly battling a porn addiction. To an outsider looking in, this didn't seem to be the case. No one would've noticed, because my ability to mask my emotions and put on the façade of perfection had become my greatest hobby.

The key word here is "seemed." *Seemed* is an interesting word because it's based on what a person "saw." This feeds into assumptions deriving from a set of behaviors and principles based on one's own perception of the situation. Thus, perception is the key to understanding that "everything is not always as it seems." Let me further explain how something as simple as perception can be detrimental to one's mental health.

They saw I had graduated, had studied abroad, and did phenomenal work overseas . . . but little did they know that I was suffering from panic attacks that forced me to believe everything bad would happen in a moment. Have you ever experienced such deep insanity that you become scared of yourself, your thoughts, and your own body, and fearful that you had no control over any of it? Yeah, that was me.

A relative expressing their congratulations told me, "Wow, Ashley, I'm so proud of you. You're doing so good in life. You're conquering the world, girl. Go ahead!"

Conquer the world, I thought. *I can barely conquer my own thoughts.*

Little did they know, I was battling depression—or rather, I was ruled by depression, for the enemy had managed to take over the majority of my mind. It was so much so that he altered my perception of myself, completely shattered my confidence, and left me with doubt, insecurities, and fear. The insecurities were so bad that I skipped classes daily because of my fear that I would never reach the level of my white colleagues—despite the fact that these were people that I'd already been taking classes with for four years, and had previously never felt such sentiments toward.

They saw I was a "good child." Coming from a Caribbean family, being a "good child" somehow equates to you being able to do nothing wrong.

Little did they know, pornography became my entire search history. My addiction overcame my desire to do anything else. I would say, "Okay, after this video, I'm done." Three videos later, I'd be saying, "Oh, this is good, I just have to finish." Some days, I would watch porn all day, causing me to miss opportunities, classes, and my responsibilities. That's how deep I was in. My potential, intellect, and capability were being sucked out of me, as I was constantly in a trance, completely ignoring other things in my life.

This later transformed into sex, as I developed an un-satisfied appetite. Incubi and other sexual demons would taunt me constantly. Being ignorant of spiritual things, I just assumed that I was just human, with normal sexual desires. I can assure you, those were not normal or human, nor were they acceptable. They took over my life—and that is not God's desire for sex. Sex is supposed to be something beautiful, not destructive. I can tell you now, those demons didn't just come from nowhere. The door had to be opened for them to enter my life, possibly from all of the sexually suggestive music, and definitely from all of the porn.

Can you now see how one "small sin" can manifest itself into a bigger problem and open the door for other sins to enter easily? You may think something is not that deep, but in reality, problems that you ignore continue on into your future. This "small" problem affected my relationships and became something I had to deal with later on. In all honesty, if I were still addicted to porn, I would have missed out on so much in my life; I would not be where I am today.

To understand how good God is and how far He's brought me, it helps to see the depths of the pit that broke me.

THE BREAKING POINT

"To break" means to have an interruption of continuity or uniformity. The key word there is *interruption*. An interruption had to occur in order to uproot my old, mediocre ways and replace them with new desires—desires not for material objects, but rather solely for things concerning God. At the time, I was not searching for God at all. Unbeknownst to me, God was crucifying my old desires of lust, victimization, deceit, and manipulation, pruning me to be the woman I was called to be. Little did I know that this was a part of His plan all along . . . to transform my life from the inside out!

After months of struggling, I finally opened my mouth and told a friend. In December 2017, this friend called me unexpectedly during the Christmas season. She's a good friend, but she wasn't a best friend. She randomly Facetimed me and, while I was speaking to her, my spirit was urging me to take a leap of faith and share. My spirit confirmed that she was a source that I could rely on. So when she asked how I was doing, I left the living room where my family was and went up to my room to tell the truth about the depression I was experiencing. This is the part that gets a little fuzzy in my memory. I don't remember exactly what she said, but I do remember it being centered around God. I remember her saying, "I will pray for you." I didn't think too much of it because during this time I was a lukewarm Christian thriving in sin. So I just smiled and thanked her.

I still to this day don't know if she actually prayed for me; all I know is that, day by day, I started to get glimpses of light.

My recollection of time during this season is a complete blur. Days or maybe a week later, I opened the Bible and couldn't put it down. I couldn't get enough. This was a major transformation for me, because I never really studied the Bible in such a way as I was now. Before that moment, I only read in church or when my deacon of a father would ask when the last time was that I opened my Bible. Little did I know, I was unintentionally in deep study, becoming a lover and a scholar of the Word. I started to smile again.

Even though I was left alone in my pit, dealing with panic attacks, depression, and isolation, the Bible became my light, guiding me out of the pit. Then I saw another, physical light reaching, pulling me out—my mother, who encouraged me to take my mental health seriously, because far too many people in my community do not.

You may be thinking, wow, I never thought Ashley went through anything like this. I would've never guessed. Or you're probably thinking, why is she telling me this? Truthfully, these sentiments were not easy to write. However, before I wrote this chapter, God revealed to me that this needed to be done to break generational curses. I cried in fear, then realized that, in order to free myself from the wickedness that once covered me, I must become comfortable sharing my *entire* testimony. With the opening of our mouths and the sharing of our stories, God is glorified and more souls are set free!

Thankfully, after time in that dark place, alone, waiting for someone to save me, I received supernatural, spiritual healing by none other than God. I was able to overcome these demons, which left me able to receive the messages to come.

After a season of daily waking up early to read the Bible, a shift occurred in my mental, physical, spiritual, and emotional state. The best way to describe it is from Romans: "Don't change yourselves to be like the people of this world, but let God change you inside with a new way of thinking. Then you will be able to understand and accept what God wants for you" (Romans 12:2a, ERV).

Indeed, God had done a complete 180 in my life. I did not ask for it, but in my studying of the Word of God I started to receive revelations on why the sin I was deeply embedded in was so wrong. I no longer had the desire to get drunk or party. I was content with staying home on Friday night, studying the Word of God. Not too long after this season began, I decided to go deeper, to offer up my body and start my path to celibacy.

The next level required submission before my elevation. All I had to do was offer up my heart, and in all of my brokenness He received me and transformed my entire life. **God wanted nothing from me, but He wanted to liberate me from myself.** I was receiving blessings that I didn't seek. God was restoring the confidence the enemy had stolen and was eliminating the insecurities the enemy had given. In doing so, God was able to reveal things I didn't know existed.

My testimony taught me that my life as a Christian before 2017 was mediocre. I was a basic chick claiming to love God, but I was not filled with the Holy Ghost and was trying to fill a hole that only God can fill. I was not a real Christian. I had no power behind my prayers. Real Christians have power. Power to manifest changes in their life. Power to work miracles and change situations in the earthly realm by tapping into the spiritual realm. Real Christians don't focus on religion; they focus on relationship. To us, God is not a genie. To us, God is our provider, healer, miracle worker, friend, and uncon-ditionally loving Father.

How do you repay One that loves you unconditional-ly, despite your flaws? You submit to Him, you obey, and you offer your life as a living sacrifice.

Now, the great thing about being mediocre is that there is always a next level to ascend to. And the great thing about God is that it's never too late. So let me fur-ther explain this concept of mediocrity so we can really understand how to go deeper in Christ.

DON'T BE BASIC

We've all heard the saying "don't be basic." According to Urban Dictionary, "basic" is a person that cannot make their own decisions and likes whatever is mainstream. Today, being "basic" is an insult. So why, when it comes to the things of God and the Word of God, are we content with being mediocre? Or, in a more colloquial way, with being basic?

Why do we only go to church on Sundays? Why do we only pray on *Sundays*? Why is the only time we open a Bible on SUNDAYS? And why do we only talk to God when we need something, and if we don't need anything that week, then why do we only talk to God *on Sunday*? When I was growing up, my teachers would always tell my mother that "Ashley is passing, but she's doing the bare minimum—just enough to get by." As I reflect on our society, this bare minimum, mediocre, "just enough to get by" attitude is the same as the one taken with our relationship with Christ. Rather than a relationship, it's more like a routine. We pray because it "seems like" what we need to do to go to Heaven. We go to church because it "seems" like what we need to do to get to Heaven.

I am here to tell you that the days of saying "I'm just a Christian" just won't suffice. In order to secure our spot in heaven, *we must go deeper* in Christ through real, authentic relationships with Christ. Your relationship will help you through tough times, help you have faith in the unseen, and ground you when everyone else fails you.

Besides, the world is watching. They're watching to see how Christians respond in times of chaos, life, and death.

As a Christian, what are you doing in your life that is ill-reflective of the God you serve? How are you responding when things hit the fan? Do you turn to God or alcohol? What have you become a slave to, or allowed to seep into your life, that has no right being there?

If you want others to take God seriously, you must first do so in your own life. Even as I am writing this chapter, God is reminding me that I need to keep practicing discipline in my life.

We make a commitment to give up our lives, sacrificing ourselves to Christ and accepting Jesus as our Lord and Savior. I strongly believe that there must be a mental shift when it comes to our responsibilities as Christians. Many times, we believe that our only goal is to get to Heaven. Yes, that should be a goal; however, did we forget that Jesus went around evangelizing, healing the sick, praying for people, and saving souls for the Kingdom of God? We must act with intentionality and remember the very reason for which we decided to give our lives up to Christ. We must tap into that Holy Ghost power that is within us and elevate our lives.

This should be our approach when it comes to our Christian lifestyle. The Jesus approach. As Jesus is, so are we, in this world!

It's time for generational curses of mediocrity in Christ to be broken. No longer should I, my family, or anyone connected to me be bound by curses that are swept under the rug, unspoken, or dealt with in silence. This is the sacrifice for freedom.

GO DEEPER (YOU HAVE NOTHING TO LOSE BUT YOUR CHAINS)

Heart check: Evaluate your heart. Don't lie to yourself. Is your heart pure?

Free yourself from anything and everything holding you back from fully pursuing God: My best way of explaining this is through a prayer . . .

Dear Father God, we come before You today with an eagerness to learn more. Lord God, I come before You today just as I am. I know I have strayed from You for a while, but I'm here, desperately and anxiously seeking You. This time, I want to go deeper. Father, prune me of my ways and of anything that exists in this flesh that is unlike You. All of the pain and heartache of my past, I offer up to You. Release me, Lord. I want to encounter You in a new way today.

Quit the basic, routine prayers you've been praying since you first started talking: Go deeper in your prayers. Personally, I am constantly working on being fully honest with God because He already knows our true heart and what we're going to say before we say it. Talk to God like you talk to your friends—besides, it's a relationship. Go to Him with gratitude for all your blessings and, in the same breath, all your pain and struggles.

Seek God daily: The most beautiful thing about serving an unseen God is that you see Him daily, whether it be through friends, family, dreams, signs, or strangers you meet. God lives within each and every single one of us. Seek Him and you will indeed find Him.

Read, study, and meditate on scripture. Apply it, then allow scripture to transform and renew your mind: It's simple; read the Bible.

Stop blaming God for bad things that have happened in your life: As Christians, we are not exempt from struggles, trials, or tribulations. However, we have the spiritual weaponry granted through God to combat these.

Seek deliverance: The way my life manifested itself was not due to random circumstances. Things that were in my life were there because I had opened up a door for demonic influences to enter. Without shutting that door, they had free reign on my soul. This is why deliverance is important. In order to truly be free from these things, we must be delivered.

The moral of the story is this: just when we think about giving up because we're experiencing what seems to be the worst moments of our lives, oftentimes, God is actually pruning us to experience a next level. Rather, think of the experience as a part of your soon-to-be testimony.

Turning Point

Crystal M. Adair

"When I don't know what else to do, I do what I do best . . . I push people away. I suppose in that void I can find some quiet. Not always answers. Or clarity. Or even peace. But I'll at least find quiet—a counter to the deluge and the cacophony of voices that live inside of my head. These voices are loud, obtrusive, and uninvited . . . But compartmentalizing [them] is not as easy to do anymore. After 44 years, there exists no more space inside of myself—no more nooks and crannies in which to tuck away my lost-ness or dis-ease. These pockets are full now, and I don't want to cry anymore. I don't. I just want for them to leave—the squatters, the voices, this deafening cacophony. It's either them or me . . . and I can't go just yet."

Six weeks into quarantine.

On a Sunday morning in April.

I sat penning those words on the backside of an old Pepco envelope while sobbing uncontrollably.

NO OTHER GODS BEFORE ME

Sometimes, I feel like that same seven-year-old girl who's clinging to her adopted mother's coattail and waiting to be rescued. My mother once said that she saw me "sinking" into her bedroom floor. It was as if I was being swallowed by quicksand, she described. So, without hesitation, she yanked me onto the bed, plopped me down beside her, and then hollered at the hardwood planks.

"You can't have her," she bellowed, "She belongs to me—not you! I rebuke thee Satan in the name of Jesus! Glory Hallelujah!"

You see, my mother could "see things" that I could not. But I never worried. I never feared. Mommy was always there to cover me, to protect me—like a deity. In my 2017 memoir, I wrote, "There was safety in [her] words. Not like the shelter of four walls and a roof—but more like the promise of God that He will never leave you or forsake you. And because she was my God for so long, I am still twisted about religion to this day." But now, I'm a full-grown woman—well past the age of accountability. So it's high time that I finally understand these demons for myself.

More often than I'd like to admit, my crazies come back to visit—each of them wily, dark, manipulative, and paralyzing. I can feel them as they reemerge in my spirit. They wrench. They reverberate. They tire. They compete for my peace of mind, leaving me without any energy or strength to fight. So, I don't. On many days, I just nestle somewhere between daydreaming, sleeping, and sobbing—grieving for the past. But it isn't 1989 anymore! It isn't the day after Thanksgiving of that year. My adopted mother didn't just hemorrhage to death at Providence

Hospital. She didn't just drink herself into an early grave. All of that is in the past now, and I have to leave it there.

But I can't.

I already told you. My adopted mother wasn't just a God-send for me. She had become my God in human form. She was a God with heavy hands, a soft mound of a belly, and a mustache unlike any that I'd ever seen on a woman. My God spoke Tarheel and Gullah, and she fried fish every Friday night and cooked chitterlings and black-eyed peas every New Year's Day. For years, my adopted mother was the only God that I knew, and in truth, the only one that I ever wanted to know. After all, it was she who took me in after my biological mother had abandoned me.

I was one year old when my birth mother left me and my biological brother alone in a garage for two weeks while she binged on heroin and on no-count men, forcing my six-year-old brother to scrounge the neighborhood for scraps. When we were found, I was the "least of them"—soiled, malnourished, and with matted hair. But my adopted mother saw past all of that and still loved us as her own. It was also my adopted mother who walked in on my foster brother one night. I was about seven. She said that he was standing over top of me, "doing something he ain't had no bidness." But like a God, this woman swooped in, shooed away my perversely curious sibling, and salvaged whatever innocence of mine that remained. She was always right on time that way. This voodoo magic woman also had a way of calming me, many times without words. As a little girl, I would throw my legs over her hip and ask her to massage the soles of my feet until my eyelids grew heavy. My adopted mother never once turned me away. She always obliged.

So imagine my surprise when I recently heard the voice of God—the God of all the heavens and of all the earth—ask me a question. I was sitting by my favorite window, in my favorite chair, just before the sun was to rise over the trees and the train tracks in the distance. There I sat, quietly meditating, listening to unbothered sparrows (my mother's favorite bird), and attempting to unbusy my frenzied mind. And that's when I heard Him. That's when I heard the God that my mother had prayed to for all of those years. He asked me a simple question, albeit one that was disturbing and uncomfortably persistent.

He asked, "Do you love God more than you love your mother?"

I stammered.

"Do you love God more than you love your mother?"

"Wait . . . What?"

"Do you love Me more than you love your mother?"

"Please . . . Please, please don't ask me that," I begged Him.

I mean, why would God ask me that? How could He expect for me to choose? Why were my loyalties even in question? There was no way—no way—that I could ever decide between my earthly, fleshly God, who I loved more than life itself, and the One who hung the stars in the sky and parted the Red Sea. I was dumbfounded by God. Without words. Dare I say, offended. I was befuddled as to what God was trying to prove.

So, I did what many of us would do.

I questioned God.

I asked God if He had forgotten. Had He forgotten who my adopted mother was for me? Had He forgotten that she saved me from my own stench? That she gave me everything that a dirty, destitute, and deserted little girl could ever want?

For thirteen years of my life, my adopted mother fed me, clothed me, tied ribbons on my pigtails before school, and rubbed my anxious, rocking feet before bed. It was this woman—this godhead—who taught me that little, chocolate-brown girls like me were beautiful too, no matter what the jealous bullies at school might say. It was this supernatural healer who loved me from a nothing into a somebody. So, again, why, God? How can You ask me to choose? How can You pit Yourself, who is God, against the only human manifestation of God that I'd ever seen with my own eyes?

Okay, okay. So, maybe I went too far. Maybe I was too bold, perhaps blasphemous. I didn't mean to be. I was just so tired of having to prove my faithfulness to God. Over and over again, for years on end, I've had to submit and to sacrifice something new and more painful every day. But I had already done that, right?! I had already bared my soul in my memoir. I had already confessed all of my sins and shame. I had already disclosed my most defiling secrets. So, what more did God want from me?! What more did He expect?! Now, I'm not denying Him or His goodness. I know that it's because of His grace and His mercy that I still stand. But how could I reasonably choose between Him and my mother? How?! I mean, that was an impossible, preposterous, and, not to mention, very painful question.

THE INNER MAN

Ephesians 3:16.

A Sunday morning.

The pastor preached on livestream while I wrestled in my mind. But as soon as his sermon began, I understood what God was doing. I could see what God was orchestrating on my behalf. He was using this man of God to reach me because, as Anthony Brown declares in his song "Worth," "[God] thought I was worth saving." So I commanded my soul that day to listen, to just "peace be still" and listen to the Word.

"We are blessed according to God's riches and abundance in heaven," Pastor taught, "and these riches are proportional to the power of the Holy Spirit that is working within our inner man or inner woman!"

Damn, I thought.

There's no hope for me then.

Not for me.

I'm unstable, unsure, easily distracted. Someone like me isn't strong enough to receive God's riches and abundance. I'm too weak in my spirit to receive God's bounty, and now I feel troubled—in trouble. But despite how Pastor's message may have landed, it was still good teaching. You see, when I had heard Ephesians 3:16 before, I had only reveled in its feel-good promises of heavenly riches and abundance. I had never paid attention to God's call to action: If I wanted God to show out in my life, then I first had to show up in my spirit. I suppose this explains why I haven't gotten all that I've prayed for these years. The house. The husband. The father figure for J. The salary increase. The dreams fulfilled. None of it. I just keep repeating the same cycles. Spinning my wheels in the mud. I'm not growing in Christ. I'm not bearing any fruit. But Lord knows, I'm trying. I really have tried.

For twenty-five years, I struggled with major depression. I even published a book about it. In this purging, I was careful to give God all of the praise and all of the glory. At book signings, I testified emphatically about "my breakthrough." I spoke about forgiveness and faith. I even started doing radio shows and speaking engagements because I genuinely wanted to bring as many people to Christ as I could. But was I really as free as I wanted to believe? Was I completely unshackled from my grief and isolation? Moreover, am I any closer today than I was three years ago to being who God has called me to be?

The answer, I'm afraid, is "No."

Sure, I've made gains in my life. Sure, I've been blessed. But after forty-four years, I still get lured back into the wilderness. I still feel broken. Bound. Not enough. I wear glib and gloom like a tattered overcoat that I don't want to take off. So, Pastor was right that Sunday morning. God needs for me to strengthen my *inner woman* before I can start walking in and living out my divine purpose in Christ. But in order to get to that *inner woman*, God first had to get through to my untrusting heart.

HELP MY UNBELIEF

Bing!

I was getting a text.

The atmosphere was shifting again.

Ayana was messaging me to talk shop, or so we thought. But within minutes, our text thread had turned into a phone call, and our phone call had turned into ministering. Ayana poured into me as I poured out my heart. Nobody expected the waterworks that followed, but that didn't stop them from coming. So, for the next hour, we talked about my memoir, my backstory, the voices that live inside of my head—everything! It wasn't customary for us to get so personal, even though we have genuine admiration and respect for one other. But this time was different. This time, I came to Ayana un-healed, un-whole, and un-masked. She didn't know this Crystal. But as a P.K. and a sold-out Christian, Ayana did know that I needed more than just prayer and a listening ear.

No, I needed a Word from God that would penetrate my spirit, unburden my soul—give it rest.

"Why do you have to choose?" she asked matter-of-factly. "Why can't you just love God *and* love your mother?" She made it sound so easy. "Why must one come at the expense of the other?"

Ayana pointed me next to Mark 9:24. "Read it!" she commanded like the educator she is, "Look it up!" In it, the desperate father of a sick child cries out to Jesus, "I do believe; help my unbelief!" Ayana likened that father to me. You see, Ayana knew my heart. She knew that I loved God. She knew that I was a woman of strong faith, of a tested faith. So, for her, I wasn't warring with the Lord about His question so much as I was warring with my own unbelief.

When God took away my mother, He took away nearly every reason for me to believe, because for me, her eyes were His eyes. Her hands were His hands. Her voice was His voice. The two of them were inextricably intertwined, the same. So, when God took away my mother, my relationship with Him also shifted, changed. God had decimated my ability to believe, to love, to trust anymore, as I was faced with knowing that someday people can just be ripped from your life without any warning at all.

"God knows that you love your mother," Ayana continued. "He gave you your mother! He gave you your mother to love you, to be there for you, to help and to guide you. He wouldn't ask for you to choose. He wouldn't separate you from her love."

Each word that Ayana spoke broke me down to the studs. The tears rushed again, and I wanted to believe her. Oh God, I wanted to believe her!

"God just wants for you to understand that *He* gave you your mother. *He* sent her to you. Then He used your mother to show you what *His* love was like. Girl, God loved you that much!"

Truth is, I did want to experience God's agape love. I wanted to experience it fully and unreservedly, but what guarantee did I have that it would last forever? That it would be faithful? Constant? Still, I desperately wanted to believe with my whole heart. I needed to. After all, it's hard living this life alone—always being afraid to love, shutting people out, pushing people away.

"Pray," Ayana instructed. "Just pray. Say, 'Lord, help my unbelief. I really want to believe on a deeper, more intimate level. But I don't believe like that right now. Lord, please help my unbelief.'"

Deep breath. Ayana's words had given me a peace, permission. Before then, I never knew that I could admit unbelief—out loud. I could actually tell God that I didn't believe Him sometimes, that I found it hard to love Him sometimes. I thought that I was supposed to suppress these feelings, push them down, tuck them away. But now I know that God just wants for me to show up *as I am* and to be completely honest with Him. I also know now that I can't deliver myself from this place of unbelief. I need help, and that help can only come from God.

FOLLOW ME

Two days after our conversation, I prayed Ayana's prayer in earnest.

I prayed for God to "help my unbelief."

"Lord, if there's any deeper love," I said, "a more intimate love that's possible with Christ, I want to know that love too. I believe, but help me with my unbelief." Almost immediately, God moved in that room. He stirred the atmosphere. It was as if a wind came through, picked up, and lifted away any and all debris. There was no more shame or guilt or heaviness in the air, and I felt lighter than I had in weeks. I finally had been honest with God about my unbelief, and rather than punish me, He rewarded me. I was so thankful.

But He wasn't done.

Not more than two minutes later, I opened my email, and what did I see? It was a daily devotional. It was the story of Peter. But it wasn't Peter's denial of Jesus that shook me. It was what Jesus had asked Peter when He forgave him, and it was also the calling that was on Peter's life. Jesus asked Peter not once, not twice, but three times, "Simon, son of John, do you love Me?"

Three times.

The Lord asked Peter *three times* if he loved Him.

But the Lord had also asked me *three times* if I loved Him.

Just a few weeks earlier, I had sat by my favorite window, in my favorite chair, and God had asked me thrice, did I love Him more than I love my mother? It wasn't the same phrasing as the question to Peter, I know. But I do believe that it was with the same intent. What's more, Peter's reply to Jesus' question never wavered. It was always, "Yes, Lord, You know that I love You." God needed to know Peter's heart because there was a calling on Peter's life. Each time Peter affirmed his love for the Lord, the Lord then instructed him to feed His sheep. Then, at last, Jesus said to Peter, "Follow me." Jesus knew all that Peter had done. He knew all that Peter had been through. But the calling on Peter's life was greater than any of his faults.

"Feed my sheep."

"Feed my flock."

"Follow me."

Peter was being called into ministry.

Peter was being called into ministry.

Peter was being called into ministry.

Maybe I was being called into ministry.

IT IS FINISHED

I don't eat crabs.

I don't even like crabs!

But I was captured.

Two days had passed since I had completed my first draft of this chapter, and now I was watching this cooking video on Facebook. I was watching like I knew this woman, but I didn't. I had no clue who she was. Still, for whatever reason, this woman brought me so much joy, so much familiarity. J even came over to sit next to me on the bed. "Mom, you squealed," he remarked, "You never laugh." But this woman was hilarious—her lilt, her twang, her flamboyance, her soft mound of a belly in her tight, bright yellow romper. She fought with those crabs, and they fought with her. She seasoned everything and measured nothing. She brimmed over with antics and with this deep, abiding, and soulful kinda love.

Before I knew it, I was trying to sear this woman's image into my memory. I didn't want to let go of how she was making me feel. It was as if I was sitting in that old, rickety highchair with the ripped seats in my adopted mother's kitchen in 1982. As we watched together, I remember saying to my son, "J, if you ever wanted to know what your Grandma Bernie was like, this is it."

That's when it hit me. Like a ton of bricks, it hit me.

Then, it crushed me.

For a fleeting moment, my mother's spirit had come back to visit. It had returned through this crab-fightin', colorful woman to tell me that she was okay, that it was okay for me to let go now. Bernie was showing me how she wanted to be remembered, not how she wanted to be grieved.

J must've seen the swift change in my countenance. He must've noticed the tears beginning to fall, which is why he said, "Mom, sometimes I feel bad for you." So, I excused myself to the bathroom so as not to upset him further. There I collapsed on the floor and released. Saying "yes" to God was never a one-time, defined, and lucid moment for me. It's always been a litany of somewhat ambiguous moments, where God is asking me to dig deeper—to peel back more layers. Every day, I have to say "yes" to Him just to have joy, just to stay sane, just to get out of bed in the morning! When the spirit of depression binds you, getting out of bed every day is an act of courage, of strength. Depression literally weighs you down from head to toe. Your chest cavity, your limbs, your extremities—your eyelids even—nothing wants to move. Nothing can move. Were it not for a supernatural act of the Almighty, you would literally lie there and waste away. So, for me, saying "yes" to God means dying to self every day. It means denying my flesh every day, doing the complete opposite of what my flesh is telling me.

It means getting out of bed and putting one foot in front of the other.

It means praying as I wash my face, brush my teeth. It means meditating as I sip my honey-lemon-ginger tea.

It means preaching God's Word to myself and exalting Him in praise as I drive to work.

It means turning off all of the sad love songs on the radio and changing the station to some "Way Maker" and "I Won't Complain."

It means exercising, going outdoors—feeling the Creator's sunshine on my face every day.

Daily, I must present myself to God as a willing and open vessel. I must empty myself—not of my allegiance to and affection for my mother, but of my idolatry of her. That's the only way that God can pour into me. That's the only way that He can heal me and use me for His glory.

Like Peter, there's a calling on my life.

A mighty calling.

But before answering this call and fulfilling my purpose in Christ, God first needs to know with whom I stand. Yes, God knows all that I've done. Yes, He knows all that I've been through. He even knows the unutterable pain that comes with letting go of my idols and trusting Him. But the calling on my life is so much greater than all of these—so much greater than the deafening cacophony of voices that sometimes lives inside of my head.

The Price of Yes Was Priceless

Catherine Jones

Everyone's journey in saying "yes" to God is different, but we should all end up at the same place—which is in a true relationship with Jesus Christ. In these pages, I speak from my own experience and what God has taught me thus far. I accepted Jesus Christ as my Lord and Savior at the age of seven, but after that, I feel like I was bamboozled into thinking that I was in an actual *relationship* with Him. That could not be further from the truth; it was just the beginning. I had a very long way to go.

Growing up, I had a very tough life, as I was faced with the weight of both parents' severe struggle with drug addiction. Although my grandmother did all she could to help take care of me and my siblings, I still had to grow up a lot quicker and rougher than most young people. That equated to less church and more struggle, and to depending on so many other things outside of Jesus Christ to make me happy. By the time I got to my young adult years, it was as if I were trying to make up for all of the things that I wasn't afforded as a child. I had developed such a hard wall of protection for myself and what I wanted that I even got on my *own* nerves sometimes! Everything had to be *my way*. It was all about me and having a great life. I graduated from college, was consumed by my career, began chasing money, and got entangled in a heavy party life with a sharp tongue and a one-two punch that could lay you flat on your face if you tried to mess with me. I didn't take no junk off anyone. Not even the appearance of it. My behavior was as if I were in control of my life and too busy for God. And because I was a "Christian" who was somewhat brought up in the church, I thought I was covered as far as my relationship with God was concerned. I had a Bible that I read from time to time, and I even prayed and went to church here and there, so I thought I was fine, without even taking the *time* to realize I was extremely far from the Lord. That all ended in 2016, when the guy I was dating and in love with just decided he was too busy *for me* and wanted out of the relationship. Isn't that something? I carried on as if I was too busy for God, only to have the person I wanted to be busy with turn around and treat me the way I was actually treating God. God has an interesting sense of humor.

That's when everything changed. I mean, that breakup really messed me up and put me on my knees, asking God, why?! Why is this happening to me, God? After a few sleepless nights spent praying in a dark closet, I realized that I was truly lost, and regardless of how things appeared, everything in my life was out of control. I'll never forget how, during that time in the closet, I heard God speak to my heart, saying, "Listen, Cathy, you're lost because you're out of relationship with *Me*. It's bigger than him. And until you stop this foolishness and put your trust in Me, I can't bless you to receive what I have just for you. You cannot come to Me with only the things you want Me to fix, without coming to Me about all of the other issues you have, because it's some of that *other* stuff that has contributed to you being lost. Bring it *all* to Me, so I can iron out your *whole* life, and put it back together the right way, *My way*." It was in this moment with God that He asked me if I was *willing* to move forward with Him. I said, "Yes, God," and rededicated my life back to Him. But I really had no idea what I was saying "yes" to. This is where the work started in order to build my relationship with Him. I quickly realized that there was a price to yes, by *eventually* understanding what I meant when I said it.

During this particular season of my life, I felt like I was caught up in the Matrix. I started being extremely tested by God, which caused a lot of pain and suffering. We can call this the rainy season, because all I did was cry. And it's funny: I thought since I *did* say "yes," the pain and tears from the breakup would go away and everything would just get better. But it actually felt like things got worse. I was feeling more broken, as God started showing me *my* sinful areas in the relationship with my ex, instead of helping me to feel sorry for myself. On top of that, new problems in my life started rising, one after the other! What I didn't realize was that this was God's way of closing chapters of my life and pulling me closer to Him. What I also didn't know was that I was actually suffering through part of the price of yes, which was the fact that God had to break my heart in order to blow my mind.

The price of yes is really dependent upon how a person spiritually defines "yes" to God. How you define it will detail the cost. And if you asked me what "yes" meant during that time, I wouldn't have been able to define it, because I wasn't sure what the will of God was for my life. After dusting the Bible off, getting active in church and attending regularly, and daily devoting time to Jesus Christ in prayer, the Holy Spirit started helping me to define "yes." He helped me to see that "yes" meant being in agreement with God the way it says in Proverbs 3:5-6 (NKJV), trusting in the Lord with all of my heart, and not leaning on my own understanding; in all of my ways, acknowledging Him, so that He would direct my path. Once the Holy Spirit helped me to define "yes," I was able to understand what yes was going to cost me.

When I think about the price, *for me*, Romans 12:1b–2 (NKJV) says it best. I had to present my body as a living sacrifice, holy and acceptable unto God, which is my reasonable service, and not to be conformed to this world, but be transformed by the renewing of my mind, proving the good, acceptable, and perfect will of God for my life. Overall, that was the price of being in agreement with God. So, it cost me everything because it cost me my life! I gave up everything in order to truly follow Jesus the right way.

I had to begin making sacrifices for a plan that was much bigger than myself. I couldn't just spend all the money that I made on myself because I had to sacrifice the tithe. I couldn't treat people any ol' kinda way when I felt hurt because I had to sacrifice being a witness of Christ in this world. I realized that I was on *God's* payment plan, if you will, because whether I liked it or not, there were sacrifices that had to be made. It was no longer just about me getting my wish list filled, or getting every prayer that I lifted up answered. I recognized that God was positioning me in places, situations, and circumstances where sacrifice was required to honor the greater work that God was doing beyond my selfish desires. It was the point where my responsibility to Jesus Christ and His people outweighed my desire to please myself. It was about me being a part of something bigger, something that I was willing to sacrifice for. And that *bigger* is the plan of God. So, the price of "yes" meant saying no to and giving up some things I wanted to say "yes" to, in order to live out the will of God for the glory of God, rather than living a mediocre life that I thought was best for me, which had only led to disappointment, heartache, and pain.

As I reflect on God's "payment plan" that I was on (and still am on), I realized that I needed to focus on spiritually investing and making deposits in the following three areas.

I had to spiritually invest in fervent prayer. James 5:16 (NKJV) says, "Confess your trespasses to one another, and pray for one another, that you may be healed. The effective, fervent prayer of a righteous man avails much." Any time your prayer life increases, you are forced to remove yourself from the crowd—and that's exactly what happened to me. It cost me friends and popularity. But it was what I needed in order to start spending time reading and studying the Bible, so that I could understand what God was trying to say to me in the scriptures while in prayer. It was amazing how God started teaching me the correct way of effective communication with Him. It blew my mind because I saw how He wanted me to know I was on the right track and was hearing from Him accurately by bringing what He said into existence, quickly! These are just some of the reasons that made me fall in love with Him during this time, seeing and better understanding His great love for me. I began reading the Word daily and getting scripture in me during my daily devotion. And the more time I devoted to Him in prayer, the more I realized how much I needed Him in every area of my life. He began opening up new relationships for me with people that I could pray with, individuals who I could trust with the drama, issues, and chaos of my life. This helped me to really see the type of people I needed in my life, versus those I *thought* were true friends. It's scary to look back at those individuals who I thought were my friends, who wouldn't have been able to pray me out of a brown paper bag, if need be, versus those the Lord began to place around me.

Also, by stepping up my prayer life, the Lord led me to incorporate fasting into my spiritual life, which really helped me to hear from God more clearly and deepened my convictions. This led to true repentance in my life from those things that were completely against the will of God. See, sometimes we repent because we're afraid that God is going to drop hot coals of fire on us if we don't. However, God is so good, He helped me to feel such a deep love in His presence. I wasn't repenting from sin because I was afraid of God and His wrath (although I do have a healthy fear of Him); instead, I began loving Him so much it truly hurt me to know how much it grieved Him to see me live the sinful life I was living. He showed me how much it hurt *Him* to see me hurting *myself.* I began feeling such an appreciation for how much He loves me, and how many mistakes He has forgiven me for, that all I could do was cry out during prayer in repentance. And the more He let me know I was forgiven and that He wanted the best for me, the more I cried. And the more I cried, for those reasons, the more He comforted me and gave me peace.

Paul, in 2 Corinthians 7:10a (NKJV), says that "godly sorrow produces repentance," and that is so true! I realized that, for the first time, my tears were coming from the right place. A place of love, humility, and godly sorrow, which can only come from prayer and fasting. This level of prayer truly placed me in the wilderness of my life, where I experienced for myself that God is my Rock. Not my friends. Not my family. Not my job. Not my ex. Only God! As David said in Psalm 18, the Lord is my Rock! My God is my Rock! Who is the Rock except our God? Praise be to my Rock, who is Jesus Christ. Like David, He took me from mourning to thanksgiving. It was through fasting and prayer that I was able to stand on the Rock so I could see from a much higher level where the enemy was lurking all around me, trying to stop God's will for my life. The Rock became my refuge that I could hide under, where things cooled off and I could calm down. Prayer and fasting placed me in the wilderness, which sometimes felt like a brutal place to be, but it was the best place because it stretched me and made me spiritually thirsty and hungry. Jesus said, in Matthew 5:6 (NKJV), "Blessed are those who hunger and thirst for righteousness, for they shall be filled." Prayer and fasting allowed the Lord to take me to a place where I had never been before as an independent woman, forced to trust Him and not myself, people, or things. I had to lay it all out before God so He could put my life in *His* order, placing God before everything and everyone else in my life. Was it difficult? Sure it was! But it was part of the payment plan, in order to learn how to sacrifice my time and appetite for the greater good, in order to begin presenting my body as a living sacrifice, holy and acceptable unto God. The more time we give Him in prayer and fasting, the closer we get to Him.

From a humility perspective, a more fervent prayer life also helped me to see myself the way God saw me. Because God puts a big ol' mirror without smudges (the Bible) in your face and lets you see yourself in the way you look to Him, compared to Jesus Christ. And that ain't *never* pretty. It causes you to be humiliated before the Lord. It's like God was saying to me, "Since you think you're so cute, and you got it going on, and the issue is everyone except you, let Me show you what you really look like." But it's necessary because it blesses you to humble yourself before God and people. The Bible will check you; and we all need to check ourselves from time to time. This is why a different level of prayer and fasting has to come first, or else you will never trust Him enough to let God do this, not realizing it's meant to help you, not hurt you. So, fervent prayer and fasting blessed me in a major way, because it brought me to a place of full dependency on God, increased my faith in Him, and forced me to repent and humble myself, which restored my relationship with Jesus Christ.

I had to trust the process. The second deposit I had to make was placing my trust into this unfamiliar and uncomfortable process that God had me going through. I remember one day, my pastor asked me to do something I didn't want to do. I went whining to God, and He said, "Cathy, trust the process, because trusting the process means trusting Me." This is really where submission comes in. Part of submitting and putting my trust in God meant trusting the people He placed me under. He slowly began adding new people to my life to make up for the subtraction of the wrong ones. And that's scary, especially if you're like me, where you've experienced being hurt and picked on by people who you trusted in the past. This step really forced me to be vulnerable. I truly wrestled with vulnerability due to the tough shell I had built up against people in general. During this time, there was a particular woman who I seriously disliked based on my first interactions with her—only to realize that she was part of the process. Her hurtful ways challenged me to not act out as I would have normally because of my desire to please God. So, at those times when I honestly wanted to use the worst words that I could think of to address her, and maybe even add some hand action, I knew I had to surrender the situation to God. He had placed her in my life at a time when I was most vulnerable and still growing in this particular area for me to learn how to behave in these situations. So, for God, it was perfect timing because He knew what I needed in order to build a Christ-like character. I had to trust that He would fight my battles, and that not every action required a response. Michelle Obama said it best: "When they go low, we go higher." I was no longer willing to fight for myself, so I began tapping into the Holy Spirit to control myself and to trust God. And it's in such times that *only* God can help you, by helping you to see situations from His perspective. Because He isn't going to just show you them, He is going to show you where you are wrong as well, to teach you how to quickly forgive and not be so quick to point fingers at other people. I began realizing that God isn't just displeased at those who do us wrong; He is just as displeased at the negative ways in which *we* respond. And I was the Queen at being able to respond. I may not have started a lot of things, but I sure did know how to finish them. So, the process helped me to see people and relationships with others differently, in the sense that it's not always *them*, that I can be just as wrong and in need of God's forgiveness. So, watch how He works: That particular woman that I disliked? Based on a change in character, through God's process, not only are we now great friends, but I and this particular person have also been able to come together to do some powerful things in ministry for the glory of God! Praise Jesus for the process!

Through it all, I became spiritually stronger, and I saw how everything I had gone through, including that breakup with my ex, was working together for my good. That breakup, for example, blessed me and caused me to thirst more for Jesus, and I found drink. Because of trusting God's process, everything that was meant for evil, God used to bless me to move into a place of deliverance in areas of my life where I didn't even know I was in chains and bondage. That breakup was one of the best things that has ever happened to me in my life, because it placed me at the feet of Jesus Christ—and I can't imagine a better place to have ended up now that I see the results.

I had to tap into and put on the mind of Christ. We are told in 1 Corinthians 2:16 (NKJV), "For 'who has known the mind of the Lord that he may instruct Him?' But we have the mind of Christ." When I said "yes" to God, I saw it as a vow, a covenant, a commitment, like a marriage to God, and I wanted to remain faithful to that "yes" forever. So, for me, putting on the mind of Christ was the most critical for having lasting results. This is still a daily, conscious effort, because it's easy to get distracted with the ways and things of this world. Putting on the mind of Christ meant following Colossians 3:2 (NIV), setting my mind on things above, not on earthly things. I had to start exercising Matthew 6:33 (NKJV), seeking first the kingdom of God and His righteousness, so that all the other things that I needed from God would be simply added to my life. I had to set my mind on the Father's business, doing things for the glory of God and not myself, seeking righteousness and the wisdom of God, which is pure, peaceable, gentle, approachable, merciful, fruitful, steadfast, and sincere. I had to daily seek and set my mind on the fruit of the Spirit, which is love, joy, peace, patience, kindness, goodness, faithfulness to God, gentleness, and self-control.

This was difficult because it forced me to ask for and desire things of God in prayer for my overall life in general, versus the things I was used to wanting and focusing on, the things that used to control my mind and thoughts. Instead of asking for more money, I had to learn to ask for and desire wisdom from God to be a good steward of what He had *already* blessed me with. And guess what? My money started growing by default. It's like Solomon, in 1 Kings 3:5–14; when God gave him the assignment of being king, God told Solomon to ask for *anything* and He would give it to him, and Solomon asked for wisdom. And God said, "Because you have asked for *this* thing and have not asked for long life, riches for yourself, or the life of your enemies, but have asked for yourself to have wisdom to do what I have asked you to do, I'm *also* giving you what you have *not* asked for. I'm going to make you the wisest man over anyone who has come before you or who will come after you, and I'm adding on riches and honor!" Solomon had sought *first* the kingdom of God and His righteousness. And that's what I began to do. This isn't something that I did just once; I had to have a made-up mind about God and His desires, no matter *what* the enemy tries to serve me throughout life.

When I sit back and reflect on the price of "yes," I think of Isaiah 43:1b–3a (NKJV), where God says, through the prophet Isaiah, "Fear not, for I have redeemed you; I have called you by your name; you are Mine. When you pass through the waters, I will be with you; and through the rivers, they shall not overflow you. When you walk through the fire, you shall not be burned, nor shall the flame scorch you. For I am the Lord your God." I'm so grateful that He brought me through. When I look back at what affected me the most in the breakup with my ex, it was the fact that he was someone of high authority in the church, so I trusted him to live a life pleasing to God; this *should have* been observable in the way he treated others, including me, but that wasn't the case. The way he left me could have destroyed me, *but God* brought me through the fire. My life today is beyond what I could have ever dared to imagine for myself. Because I put my love for God and His will first, my relationship with Him is strong, my ministry is on the rise, I'm walking in my calling, I live in a beautiful home, my career is better than ever, and my relationships with friends and family are so much healthier. I'm not the same Christian I used to be because of God's payment plan that allowed Him to do a great work in me and make everything in my life align correctly. And that's *priceless*.

Growing up, no one talked to me about what it meant to say "yes" to God. Unfortunately, it took me reaching my thirties to say it and mean it. This is why I said "yes" to sharing my journey on these pages. Maybe my story will help someone else say "yes" to God a lot sooner rather than later. It's not easy, but it's beyond worth it. It's not an accident that you are reading these pages. God wants to do something so awesome in your life for a purpose that's greater than you. I pray you will say "yes" to God, price and all. Your life will never be the same. It'll be better. Amen.

The Courage of Yes!

Inga Robinson

When my son was born, my husband and I wanted to protect him from all the evils of the world. We wanted everything to be perfect. But like all parents, we soon learned better. One day, when James* was a toddler, he wanted to reach for a glass on our table. I warned him not to, saying, "James, don't touch or I will tap your fingers." My child-training philosophy was to give the direction and warn of the consequences first, as all decisions have consequences and repercussions. Therefore, James had a choice: to obey or receive a tap. Well, James looked at me with a scowl, pointed his little finger at me, and babbled and said, "NO!" What?! I was trying to protect him from getting hurt! After all I had done to secure his safety and care for his needs, how could he utter the word *no*? Why? After all the sacrifices, guidance, provisions, and love his dad and I had shown, why would James refuse to say "yes"? Why wouldn't the child say a resounding "yes"? It's because James found power in saying "no."

This memory brings to my imagination how God must feel about His creation, man and woman. The Bible tells us in Genesis that God formed us from the dust of the ground and breathed into our nostrils the breath of life, and we thus became a living soul. Here we are, man and woman, standing before our Creator, God the Father. Just like new parents, God's desire is to love, provide for, and protect us. He tells us so in Philippians 4:19 (NKJV): "… God shall supply all your need according to His riches in glory by Christ Jesus." But we seem to still have a child-like attitude toward God our Father. We seem to believe that the word "no" is the right answer. Like a young child, we exercise free will by saying "no." But since our Father God is seeking to care for our every need, why don't we reply with an exuberant "yes"?

Perhaps the answer starts with a scripture in 1 Corinthians 13:11 (NKJV): "When I was a child, I spoke as a child, I understood as a child, I thought as a child; but when I became a man, I put away childish things." So, the first question is, when will I grow up and stop doing childish things? It's easy to assume that with age comes maturity, but that assumption is not always correct. Rather, maturity is the point at which one is fully developed in character. Second, will my maturity (development) create a "yes, God" spirit? Maturity is gained through experiences. I am still experiencing life and developing every day. My life has been a journey of unexpected twists, turns, peaks, and valleys. However, I pray in the name of Jesus Christ that by sharing portions of my experiences, you will be strengthened in your life's journey.

I am the oldest of four children, three girls and one boy, born into an African-American middle-class family in Washington, DC. Decades before, the neighborhood I grew up in was all white, mostly Italian Catholics. Most parents were college-educated professionals and/or entrepreneurs. My father was a business owner and my mother was a teacher. I never really thought much about my future plans, because the expectations were clear—school, college, married, kids, repeat. Oak trees shaded the streets as we safely played in the wide alleyways until the streetlights came on. The single-family homes lined the block with freshly manicured lawns. As my house sat on a corner lot, strategically placed bushes marked the end of the property. In the summertime, the neighborhood had the sweet aroma of honeysuckle, mulberries, and grapes. I never wanted the summer to end. My perfect life. Right?

One afternoon, our parents piled my siblings and me into the car for a ride. They started talking about their marriage. I could not understand a word they were trying to say until finally, my father said, "Your mother wants a divorce."

"A what?" I said. I was stunned. I had more questions than answers. My perfect life was shattering. Why was this happening to my family? I did not know anyone who had been divorced. What would my friends and neighbors think? My head was spinning like a top. My grandparents weren't divorced, nor my aunts and uncles. I thought, someone has to come and talk to my parents to end this nonsense.

Unfortunately, the situation got gravely worse. Their internal fighting intensified to the point that my siblings and I were secondary to them winning the fight. My mother eventually left the home and I became "Inga and the kids." You see, I had to become the caretaker for my siblings. I remembered hearing a story once about what happens when little chicks lose their mother: the chicks will either scatter or huddle together out of fear. So, I corralled them in. I was determined that we were not going to be the "poor little Johnson children," nor the talk of the neighborhood.

The upheaval of not having my mother present was chaotic, to say the least. And at the time I didn't realize that I had been trained by my mother for such a time as this, to take care of the house and my younger siblings. The position of "Inga and the kids" placed me in a precarious position: being a child, but expected to perform adult duties; trying to preserve my childhood while being thrust into a sister/mother role. I felt that failure wasn't an option. Consequently, I developed an almost debilitating fear of failure. Somehow, I felt that I must project an image, a template of sorts, for my siblings to follow. But how could I succeed, as a child, without the life experiences to navigate my own life, let alone the knowledge of how to parent? In my quest to "get it right," I overthought most decisions, which resulted in procrastination. Has fear ever paralyzed you? I have heard that FEAR is False Expectations Appearing as Real. But at that time, the fear was real.

It is true that hurt people will hurt other people. Hurt people display behaviors that make them unrecognizable to the people that once knew them. Such was the case with my parents. My jovial father became short-tempered and hostile. Moreover, my once-supportive mother began to show increased anger and animosity toward me. Their manipulation was unbearable at times. Instead of being concerned about my wellbeing or school grades, they tried to use me to take sides in their war. Due to these household conditions, I struggled to focus on school. But somehow, God had His hand on me through it all. I was acknowledged as a leader in school and remained popular as the captain of the cheerleaders, a student government representative, etc. Only my closest friends knew about my home life. To everyone else, I tried to display a sense of calm. But internally, I was an emotional wreck.

The relationship with my parents, or lack thereof, resulted in unforgiveness on my part. The same anger that they projected onto me caused me to return the favor for many years. Uncontrollable triggers from my past had control of me. One word, "no," felt like a thousand rejections. I began to rehearse in my mind all the times that I wasn't made a priority. I felt that since I wasn't treated right, I had the right to resent them. I put on a great façade to those outside of my family, but inside, I would pray to God for help every day: Please God, help me have a better relationship with my parents. It appeared that He had an answer, but was I ready to listen? God urged me to allow Him to teach me a lesson on forgiveness. But I was being rebellious. I just wanted the pain to stop.

Being raised by my father had its fair share of challenges. I didn't really understand why this arrangement happened in the first place. But the alternative, living with my mother, didn't seem any better. Due to my "Inga and the kids" title, my father and I would have some adult-type conversations, and sometimes arguments, too. One particular day, I had had enough! I needed him to explain his conduct. I insisted that we discuss how the sacrifices that he expected of me were too much. I was responsible for the everyday needs of my siblings as well as myself, including cooking, cleaning the house, doing laundry, helping with homework, and supporting their extracurricular activities. At the same time, the sacrifices I made at Dad's home resulted in my mom's resentment of me in her home. This caused my relationship with my mother to deteriorate. I was angry. After allowing me to voice my outrage, Dad began to share with me his honest and vulnerable truth. He explained how scared he was, trying to raise four small children alone. He asked me to forgive him for expecting a child my age to take on adult responsibilities. My father continued to explain that he never meant for me to be hurt and ended by thanking me for doing a "damn good job." I was stunned. It is hard to explain the healing moment I experienced that day. Something in my heart compelled me to forgive him. I realized that the process of forgiveness requires communication. We had a new start.

Now, the process of forgiving my mother would take longer because we were both still hurting and simply didn't communicate. I was still holding on to the offenses of the past. Thank God, He had a plan to cure this malady at the root source. But instead of embracing his lesson of forgiveness, I told God, "I have already dealt with the matter. I'm not bothering with it, and it's not bothering me." Much of this statement was probably my procrastination kicking in. I wasn't ready to say "yes."

I fell in love and married a wonderful man, Big Jim*. He was funny, caring, and a great dad and provider. Unknowingly, though, I carried procrastination and unforgiveness into my marriage. Within a three-year span, we had a baby boy and bought our first house. Life was good and we made big plans together. But life was about to take a nasty turn. By year six, Jim had become dependent on drugs. Our plans to grow a family and move to a bigger house began to fade. We loved each other, but the drugs made him erratic. I was so desperate to save my marriage and not end up divorced like my parents that I went to family support counseling to better understand what I needed to do to save my husband. Then reality set in when the medical staff explained that I was an enabler. A what? An enabler. By definition, an enabler is a person who by their actions makes it easier for an addict to continue their self-destructive behavior by rescuing them. Evidently, my previous learned behavior as a child/ parent made me the perfect enabler. I was a Miss Fix-It!

If my "nurture-nature on steroids" continued to fix the messes, I was in fact assisting in killing him. I prayed to God for an answer. But the answer that came back was very different than I expected.

God said: If you want to save Jim's life, you must trust Me.

How many times had I proclaimed that Jesus was my Lord and Savior, but glossed over the "Lordship" part? My immature definition of Lordship was (in my child voice) Jesus is telling me what to do. I had to tell myself to grow up. I had been praying to the Lord for a solution. It would be insane not to follow the One that I had been praying to for help.

God continued: You must divorce him.

Me: But God, I took a vow to love him and cherish him through sickness and health. He is sick. He will never understand. He will feel that I have abandoned him in his time of need. What will the family think? What will my friends think? How will I get by without money or my house? When I got married, Jesus, I said that I would never get a divorce. Are You sure?

God: Your ways are not My ways. Trust Me to protect him, your son, and you. Do you trust Me?

Me (reluctantly): Yes, God.

I had never been so afraid in my life. This leap of faith was like walking on water for me. As our bank account was depleted and the rehab attempts failed, our only option was to sell the house and get a divorce. Jim struggled.

When I looked at him, my heart bled for the man he had become. But God reassured me that He was there. My son and I prayed for him every day.

One afternoon, I got a call from a drug rehab counselor. Jim wanted me to know that he was admitting himself to an in-patient rehab, and he wanted to see me and our son before he went away. I agreed to see him. He apologized for being weak, but I encouraged him to stay strong. After many months had passed, Jim was released from the rehab center; just as God promised, he was healed and has remained clean until this day. Now, here is how God was faithful: eventually, I receive a phone call from Jim. He had a few questions on his mind about the past. Subsequently, the conversation went like this:

He asked, "Hey, how are you? I have been thinking about you. Can I ask you a few questions?"

I responded, "Sure, Jim."

"You really loved me, didn't you?"

I responded, "Yes."

"If I hadn't F'd up our marriage by doing drugs, you wouldn't have divorced me, right?"

I replied, "No, I would not have."

"Divorcing me must have been one of the hardest decisions for you?"

I responded, "Yes it was."

To my amazement, Jim continued by saying, "Thank you for saving my life."

I could hardly speak. While choking back tears, I said, "I thought you'd never understand. But if leaving meant that you would live and not die, I had to be okay with that. God promised me."

Saying "yes" to God allows Him to fulfill His promises.

By this time, I was sure that God had called me into ministry. I was nervous and excited all at the same time. I thought that when Jim got healed, I was healed too. I was ready for the next chapter in my life. But I was still carrying unforgiveness. With all surety and attitude, I told God that I was fine. Sure, my mother and I weren't friends, but I was cool with it. But I was in denial and clearly not healed at all. I was just as volatile as before. However, by that time I was wearing a "church mask" and thought I could minister. Very sternly, God told me that He could not use me the way I was. I tartly responded, "What do You mean, You can't use me like this? You just called me to ministry, and I said yes." That response should have been a clear sign that I wasn't ready. I was trying to minister with a limp. I had a ball and chain attached to me called unforgiveness. Have you ever encountered a minister with a limp? They do good work, but not to their full potential.

Somehow, trusting God to perform a miracle in someone else's life is easier than trusting God with your own issue. Yes, it is a faith issue. I wanted God to answer all my questions before I would decide to follow. However, the truth is, if God told me everything, I wouldn't need faith.

Faith is trusting the omniscient God to lead the way. My job is to follow the Lord. I had to surrender my will to the will of God. Surrender to God does not mean giving up, but rather, yielding to God. Trusting Him enough to believe Him. But if we examine the truth of the matter, in most cases, we have to first get sick and tired of being sick and tired. Then, at that point, we will comply.

Jesus' desire is for me to be free in a way that I had never experienced. You see, my previous "yes" was for someone else. But this time my "yes, God" was for me. I had to choose not to be offended. Offense is the bait of the enemy to lure us into bondage. I was sure that my unyielding ways were going to protect me from my oppressors. But in reality, I was also blocking the good, too. They say that out of the heart, the mouth speaks, so evidently, I had allowed the bitterness and resentment to infiltrate. Well, that would explain why I would get so mad when triggered in the slightest way. My heart was wounded and needed to be healed. I had given the enemy power over my emotions by refusing to forgive. I would curse and act out my anger. God reminded me of the times He forgave me. I was wrong to try to withhold grace from someone while expecting to receive grace for myself. As the Lord's Prayer tells us, "And forgive us our trespasses, as we forgive those who trespass against us." Forgiveness is a process. It is a choice, not a feeling. To be honest, I didn't feel like forgiving. But God said, "Trust Me. It will change your life."

Faith and trust go hand in hand. I needed to understand that trust is about having a relationship. So, until I
truly understood God's character, it would be impossible
to trust Him with something of value. If you have trouble
trusting God, maybe you don't know Him. I had to get re-
acquainted by reminding myself of all the times God was
there to pull me through. To help me with this process,
I made a list of the occasions that God saved me from
danger and made a way out of no way. Before I knew it,
I was thanking God that I didn't get what I deserved. I
plead with you to trust the faithful God who loves you.
The One that will never leave you nor forsake you. The
benefits certainly outweigh the repercussions.

The results of distrust can manifest in dysfunctional
behaviors such as hoarding, procrastination, control issues, fear, anger, and, in some cases, paranoia. Many of us
are stuck in dark places because we need to be delivered.
God was calling me to say "yes" while I had the chance.
When I said "yes" this time, God promised to restore me,
to deliver me, and to give me a greater capacity to forgive. You see, the journey to recovery was never about
my mother. Rather, the lessons were all about me regain-
ing my freedom. I forgave my mother and asked for forgiveness. By releasing my resentment and years of pain to
God, I was released from the triggers that threatened to
derail my life. No longer did the enemy have power over
me. I was delivered from years of bad choices caused by
fear and brokenness.

Miraculously, my "yes" caused an unexpected result. I had no idea that my siblings were also carrying the same unforgiveness. But for them, the hurt was not for themselves, but rather for the hurt they saw me carry. The divorce was devastating to me and my siblings. However, when they witnessed the transformation in me and the grace that I showed my mother, they were amazed. You see, it was because God showed unmerited grace and favor toward me that my mother and I were able to reconcile and establish a close relationship that we had never had. And my act of forgiveness compelled my siblings to choose to forgive and heal also. Forgiveness broke the chains. My family is free to love the way God had intended for us.

I adore my mother! I can say that now with all enthusiasm and sincerity. When God restores, it is not as it was; it is better than before. Just as God promised, He restored me, my relationships, and my finances.

Jeremiah 31:22 (MSG) reads, "How long will you flit here and there, indecisive? How long before you make up your fickle mind? God will create a new thing in this land: A transformed woman will embrace the transforming God!"

I urge you, saints, to make a choice. I came back from the childish and selfish "no" woman to become the transformed "Yes, God!" woman. When you say "yes" to God, you are living a life of surrender, yielding to His way and to His will. You are discovering the key to endless possibilities. You are releasing God to unimaginably bless you; God is waiting to show off. When you say "yes" to God, God is empowering you to change your circumstances. God is helping you to continually have an attitude of gratitude. God is giving you unspeakable joy.

Saying "yes" to God is not being fearless. It is being determined to go forward despite it. "Yes, God!" makes my life HIS-STORY!

Chosen by God: The Trials, the Tribulations, the Victories!

Tammeca Riley

I write résumés for a living. Oftentimes, I use words like "tapped," "selected," "promoted," "chosen," "appointed," and "hand-picked" to highlight when my clients are promoted to new positions, asked by their managers to work on special projects, or rewarded for some outstanding work or feat. When someone is hand-picked for a specific project, promotion, or purpose, it usually implies that there is a high level of trust in that person, the person is committed and reliable when it comes to carrying out the required tasks, and the outcome or end result is expected to be favorable. Before I was in my mother's womb, God already "selected," "chose," "appointed," and "hand-picked" me for many trials and tribulations—each for a specific purpose. I had to rely on God to reveal the favorable aspects of my trials and tribulations, because by myself I could not see the blessings. I eventually came to understand the purpose behind the trials and tribulations, but not until much later in life. Why did God entrust me with these trials and tribulations? I was not reliable or trustworthy. But James 1:2–3 (NASB) tells us, "Consider it all joy, my brethren, when you encounter various trials, knowing that the testing of your faith produces endurance." I did just that—considered it all joy: the trials, the tribulations, the victories. And while I did not always recognize God's presence during my trials and tribulations, God was in control of everything all along—and He still is.

The "informal" résumé of my life goes something like this: I was hand-picked by God to be the first-born child to my fourteen-year-old mother on a summer day in Newark, New Jersey. Sometimes I wonder why. Why was I the first-born child to my mom? I still do not think I know the answer. My mother did her best to care for us, even though she only had a ninth-grade education. I remember walking home from school and stopping at her job, a local fast food spot that is no longer in business. She would give me some French fries or some other food before sending me on my way home. Other childhood memories I enjoyed include spending time at my granddaddy's farm and great uncles' homes, climbing trees, riding horses, and waking up hungry in the middle of the night and watching my granddaddy fix me a peanut butter and jelly sandwich with a glass of milk to "wash it down." My aunts took us to the circus at Madison Square Garden in New York City, and to the movies in downtown Newark after we stopped at one of the penny candy stores to buy some snacks to sneak into the movie theater. Those were some happy times, and became some of the great memories I hold close to my heart.

I was selected by God to experience constant instability in my life. The hardships of my childhood involved one common theme—instability. It took years before I would experience true stability. Only God's plan could have set my testimony in motion at the tender age of eight years old. He was preparing me for what was to come. "'For I know the plans I have for you,' declares the Lord, 'plans to prosper you and not to harm you, plans to give you hope and a future'" Jeremiah 29:11 (NIV). Before the constant instability began its full reign, we had a brief period of stability when my youngest brother's father took care of us. Although he never married my mother, I considered him to be a father to me. That brief period of stability was interrupted because of one "adult" reason or another, however, and instability returned for most of the rest of my childhood. Unbeknownst to me at the time, instability would also play a significant role in my adult life.

By the time I was eight years old, my mother was introduced to and became addicted to drugs—which was the beginning of significant instability in my life. We lived in an abandoned house in a small town in Virginia, not far from North Carolina. Fortunately, the boarded-up windows shielded us from harsh weather and it was relatively warm. When it did become colder, we stayed warm because of the heat emanating from a working stove. Eventually, we moved back to New Jersey—but without my mother, because she entered rehab as a recourse for illegal activities perpetuated by her addiction. My transient childhood continued in New Jersey when my mother returned as a recovering addict. My mom did her best to take care of us, feed us, and keep a roof over our heads.

I remember going to the store, sometimes with rolled up coins, a note, or food stamps, which were the equivalent of the modern-day EBT card or SNAP benefits. We were recipients of federal government food programs to low income households in the 1980s. My mother had a job here and there, and when we could we stayed in an apartment. Unfortunately, she was not always able to keep up with the rent, so we stayed until we were near eviction or evicted.

I was in a different elementary school practically every year of my childhood. I can only recall the first names of just a few of my friends from my elementary school years. Despite moving around and changing schools often, Mom made sure we went to school every day. My mother instilled in us the importance of education from a very young age, because she was living the struggle, first-hand, of being without a high school diploma. She felt every bit of the pain that accompanied what may, to her, have felt like inadequacy. My mother did not want her children to experience the same plight. I just knew in my heart that finishing high school and going to college were really my only options, although the circumstances leading up to my college career were quite unconventional.

God blessed us with a mother that also understood the importance of faith. Mom must have recalled Proverbs 22:6 (KJV): "Train up a child in the way he should go: and when he is old, he will not depart from it." She sent us to Sunday School and to Vacation Bible School during the summers—even when she did not go to church with us. At one point, the one single constant in my life was attending church. Later in life, my conscious and sub-conscious faith became the foundation that would carry me through adversities. I knew I could pray, no matter what was going on in my life, and God would hear me. I continued to pray even when I was not going to church. I am very transparent in my prayers. Why are we fake with God? He already knows everything, remember? He's omniscient—all knowing and all seeing. I always have a transparent, conversational prayer with God and pour it all out to Him. I do not want any confusion about why I am praying, what I am asking, or why I am thankful. This does not mean all my prayers are answered. While growing up, my prayers were very selfish—"God, please let me get that teal Adidas suit. God, please let me get the new Fila sneakers." Whew! I loved that teal Adidas suit. But I also thanked God for the blessings I recognized in my life. Sometimes we are unable to clearly see all of our blessings, especially when we are deep in the thick of our trials and tribulations. We must learn to recognize God's blessings in everything, in every situation, in every af-fliction. Whether we feel our situations are difficult, easy, big, or small, blessings are still present in the difficult, easy, big, and small situations; and those are blessings we do not deserve.

We had a period of stability and we were able to stay in one house for longer than one school year, but that was the last period of stability for us. Meals became few and far between, my mother had a relapse, and we were evicted, again. I was in high school at the time. For the remainder of my high school years, God blessed me with a friend who invited me to stay with her family, enabling me to stay in the same high school and neighborhood where many of my friends were. I felt like I had some stability again. But while my high school years had many blessings, they were also filled with troubles that I created. I did not have academic problems. My grades were just fine, which was a blessing. I had great teachers and a committed guidance counselor who made sure I took the SAT and completed applications for colleges and scholarships. I even considered joining the military. I was determined to have some stability in my life. But choosing stability for my adult life did not change my behavior during my teen years. While in high school, I only had one relationship that I would consider to be a "serious" relationship, and I managed to mess that up by creating instability and engaging in promiscuity, which was enabled by some "un-relationships." How did I get there? I did not know at the time. In hindsight, I realize that I sought out comfort in a space that I was familiar with—the instability space—even though I despised being in that space. I did not understand my state of mind during my teen years. It took years for me to recognize and understand what I did to myself and why.

After the last eviction, I was deemed a ward of the court since my mother was no longer my legal guardian.

God was setting me up for a blessing, but I had no idea it was in the works. Although there was nothing great about the circumstances surrounding why I became a ward of the court, the result of that situation was a blessing—a free education. While I was in search of stability in my life, God blessed me with the opportunity to attend college and earn a degree, for free. While I was in college, however, my mother passed away. I felt like I was thrown back into instability. I did not know where I would end up. I still did not have my life all planned out. I just desired some stability, some safety, some comfort.

Where was my father during all of this? Not having my father in my life significantly contributed to my instability. When I was around eleven years old, I was shown a newspaper article about my father, stating he was facing murder charges. I do not know all of the circumstances around my father's conviction, but when I became an adult and developed a relationship with him, he expressed his innocence and anger toward the "un-justice" system. I talked to my father about his lack of financial and emotional support for my brother and me before he was sent to prison. I explained to him that I believe his absence and lack of support were the reason we struggled, and it may be the exact reason why he is suffering now. There are always consequences for our actions—good or bad. As I am writing this, my father does not believe in God because of where he is spending his life. I revealed to him that he was not without fault in his situation. I also reminded my father that Jesus Christ was without fault when He was crucified. Then I asked him, why does he think he is blameless in his plight? My prayer for my father is that he will accept Jesus as his Lord and Savior before he leaves this earth.

I was chosen by God to experience depression. After graduating from college, I ended up getting a job and an apartment, meeting a man, and having a little girl. After the birth of my daughter and a bad breakup, I became depressed. So many questions crossed my mind. I felt inadequate, unwanted, and unstable. I felt like a failure. When things began to appear uncertain or questionable—unstable—I reacted. Unfortunately, this backfired, as either I did not have the best reactions or my timing was not great.

I relocated to another state, searching for stability, and I convinced myself that I would find it. Anxiety kicked in a few years after I relocated. I had to deal with a double-edge sword, health wise. I suffered from anxiety stemming from depression. I could not work and sometimes I could not take care of my daughter. My daughter was such a blessing—so independent and confident. There were times when I couldn't get myself out of bed, and my little girl, at five or six years old, would fix herself a sandwich for dinner while I slept. She never burned down the house and she was not afraid. To this day, she always says "I was Matilda," referring to the movie and book character that was an extremely smart and independent little girl. At bedtime, my daughter would just lie down next to me and go to sleep. At some point in the night, I would wake up and turn off all the lights and televisions and crawl back into my bed next to her.

My brother and some beautiful faith-filled people in my circle helped me and prayed for me during that period of my life. I sought treatment, went back to work, enrolled in graduate school, and started seeking out connections with men. Seeking—that was one of the biggest mistakes I made in my life. The Bible explicitly states, "He who finds a wife finds what is good and receives favor from the Lord" (Proverbs 18:22, NIV). After dealing with more of those "un-relationships," I finally decided it was time to focus on the one relationship that mattered—my relationship with God. Eventually, I was "found" by my husband—stability. But I was not always certain I had stability, because, like in most marriages, we had quite a few conflicts. I hung onto what God promised, trusted Him with my marriage, and just stuck with it. I prayed and cried during the stable and unstable times, praying that the stable phases were not just phases and that the unstable phases were just that—phases that would go away quickly. In fact, I created some of those unstable phases because of my fears. It sounds ironic, but I feared instability, which caused me to create what I feared the most by trying to be in control of it—it was the textbook version of fight or flight. I did not want to flee, so I fought . . . I disputed everything that was "wrong" in my sight.

Again, I felt inadequate, unwanted, and unstable. I felt like a failure. But God! I thank God for blessing my husband and me—two committed and forgiving souls—with each other. We were committed to our marriage and each other. Then the time came when I had no choice but to relent because cancer showed up in my life.

I was appointed by God to suffer from breast cancer. I found a lump in my breast in December 2017. That time of year was exciting for me because my daughter and I were going to see *Hamilton* on Broadway. I kept the lump a secret until after our outing to New York City. I wanted to enjoy the time with my daughter because I honestly did not know if it would be our last adventure for a long time, or forever. We visited Central Park, the Empire State Building, the Plaza Hotel, and the 9-11 Memorial. We took pictures and did a lot of talking. I did everything I could do to make sure we had good memories, just in case we were not graced with another opportunity like that again.

At the beginning of the new year in 2018, the diagnosis of breast cancer was confirmed—just like that—with no family history and no presence of the breast cancer gene. I did not know how my life, health, or family would be impacted, or how the situation would turn out. I cried, prayed, and asked God to keep me focused on Him, no matter what may be coming my way. God revealed to me: "Do not fear, for I am with you; do not be afraid, for I am your God. I will strengthen you; I will surely help you;

I will uphold you with My right hand of righteousness"
(Isaiah 41:10, BSB). As I reflected on why God chose
me to experience breast cancer, He provided me with
understanding and peace. I was not afraid. I leaned on
His promise of helping me get through yet another challenge in my life—this time a life-altering and potential
life-threatening disease.

God used the affliction of breast cancer to sit me
down. Yes, I was in time out. He told me I did not have to
worry about fight or flight because He would help me and
fight my battles. I knew God had to be glorified as a result
of this trial, so victory was inevitable, no matter what the
victory looked like. I trusted God and surrendered to His
will by believing in His victory. If God decided to grace
me with more time here on Earth with my family, that
is victory. If God decided to grace me with His presence
eternally in heaven, that is victory. I had peace in surrendering to God's will. I relented and accepted how my husband took care of our household and our sons. I experienced some rough days during treatment. Severe anemia,
low blood pressure, sickness, weakness, and weight loss
were my burdens. I recalled that Jesus said, "Come to me,
all you who are weary and burdened, and I will give you
rest. Take my yoke upon you and learn from me, for I
am gentle and humble in heart, and you will find rest for
your souls. For my yoke is easy and my burden is light"
(Matthew 11:28–30, NIV). I found rest and peace. Praise
God, I am still here and cancer-free—victory!

I am not ashamed of my hope in my Lord and Savior Jesus Christ because He has done so much for me. Psalm 25:3a (NIV) reads, "No one who hopes in you will ever be put to shame." We must experience trials and tribulations because they require us to rely on God. Relying on God through trials and tribulations will yield victories. But we must remember that those victories are for the glorification of God, and He is the only one who determines what those victories will look like. We have in our psyche that we are immune to hardships, problems, and challenges, and we have it all worked out in our minds—how and when those victories will play out. But are our versions of events aligned with God's will?

When we are chosen, hand-picked, selected, or appointed by God to endure trials and tribulations, we must surrender to His will and trust Him through it all, and He will make sure we are victorious because God must be glorified. There is always a purpose for our trials and tribulations designed by God. The revelations of my trials and tribulations were in hindsight. I did not necessarily "see" God's presence and blessings while in the midst of my experiences—while I was hungry, home-hopping, depressed, or having "un-relationships." We may not know or understand the purpose in, during, or immediately following the trials and tribulations, but eventually God will reveal to us the reasons, the purposes, and the whys. My purpose was to put all my trust in God, and, when He manifested victories, to glorify Him, praise Him, tell others about Him and what He has done for me, and share my story with the hope of encouraging others to desire their own relationship with Jesus. The Bible tells us, "Trust in the Lord with all your heart and lean not on your own understanding" (Proverbs 3:5, NIV). Relying on God and His promises—this is where I found constant stability in my life. I'm not saying it is easy, but it gets easier. In sharing with you my stories of trials, tribulations, blessings, and victories, my prayer is that you will grow in your faith in Christ Jesus through your own life-changing trials, tribulations, blessings, and victories, just as I did.

Bye, Felicia! Saying Yes to God and No to Myself

Stacy Bradner

Yes, we can. Yes, we can . . . that was the chant that roared from the crowd as the young, gifted, and black presidential candidate took his place in history. It was electrifying, and the energy was unmatched to any that I had ever witnessed in history. Confetti was all over the floor and no one cared as the rock star and his family took center stage. With hope and confidence, we said "yes" to the possibilities and to the message of the man of the hour. We were excited to turn the page with him and look forward to a new day. After all, hadn't we arrived at the destination that we had been journeying for? Wasn't this what the slaves dreamt about and Martin Luther King spoke about? But then reality set in. As good as that moment seemed, it was just a moment in time when we got behind a man, a human being. While he had swag for days, he could not maintain that place in our hearts reserved for the One that made us. Yep, he was just a man.

Often, we are more comfortable with supporting someone that we can see and touch, most especially when he looks like us. But while we may find comfort in following someone tangible, a human like us, we should not put our hope and trust in someone other than God, our Father.

What does that look like, when we affirm and exclaim that we will say "yes" to a God that we can't always see or feel, especially when He goes silent in the midst of a storm? Has that ever happened to you? Or, perhaps, you were doing everything you thought was the right thing to do. Tithing to the tenth, praying night and day, protecting your virtue, singing in the choir, serving others, and anything else you can name that made you feel righteous. And, in the midst of all your striving to live right, things were still not working out for you. How does that work? Do you continue doing the right thing? How could God allow any misfortune to even get that close to you? Isn't He supposed to be a good God that protects good people? Isn't that in the good people's contract? I do good and good things happen. Right? So, why then are you going through hardship? After all, didn't you already accept Him and, in effect, say "yes"?

Consider this an invitation to get real about the questions in your mind, so that we can get to the heart of the matter and gain the understanding of where you are and, even better, where God wants you to be. Walk with me on this "yes, God" journey, and let's explore a challenge like no other. Let's turn the page.

BYE, FELICIA!

Everyone knows a moocher like Felicia in the movie *Friday*. In my case, I know too many to count on both hands and feet. They are all around me. They need a couple of dollars, just until their paycheck. They want a place to stay until they get on their feet. They want me to cosign for their apartment. They want to call me to unload all their problems, never mind the fact that I have problems of my own. They want to put their stuff in my basement for a little while, and will even reason with me that I'm not using it, anyway. They want. They want. They want.

I can recall one person in particular who was the neighborhood nuisance. He was so annoying and needy that he would intentionally pick the most inconvenient time to ask for money so that you couldn't refuse. When people saw him coming, they would go the other way. He would normally approach late at night and out of nowhere. You felt compelled to give him something to avoid getting on his bad side and in response to the mere shock of being caught off guard. I had a strategy, though: I handled my business early, and if our paths crossed, I avoided making eye contact at any cost; after all, he was a night owl. Not.

Early one day, while I was on my way to my car for my commute to college, I was somewhat bothered because I could feel a presence. No sooner had I put my books in the back seat and swung around to open the driver's door than he appeared, coming from out of nowhere. There he was, standing in front of my driver's door, with a suit from the dry cleaners. "Give me five dollars for this suit!" he demanded. He had to be tracking me, I thought. It wasn't just the fact that he walked up so close behind me that got me, it was his appearance as well. Now, I knew him.

Although everyone said he was on crack, to me he was the guy next door, and certainly someone I looked up to at one point. He was a football star and got a scholarship to play in college. Yet, there he was, standing in front of me and blocking my door. Skin and bones. Probably six foot two and weighing no more than about 110 pounds soaking wet. His hands were shaky and he looked disheveled, with eyes wilder than midnight.

Was he really offering me a suit for five dollars at seven in the morning, one that he had probably stolen from who knows where? So, why didn't I run the other way or just jump in my car? Anybody looking that desperate would probably have asked for my car, or better yet, my wallet. I know it's crazy, but I stayed there for a second to see what would happen next. I wasn't sure I had ever let anyone in his condition get that close to me. His eyes were pleading and begging for help and I felt compelled to stare. What I really wanted to know was what had happened to the star athlete that everyone thought would make something of himself—and yet, now he looked like he was near death. I should have yelled or cussed him out, but all I could say was, "Bye, I have to go to school." He moved out of the way. That was a close call, I thought. It could have gone another way. I kept asking myself later, don't you understand that people on crack can't help themselves? And, more importantly, why didn't I offer him some words of encouragement? I promised myself that the next time, I would use more wisdom. But, what does that mean?

That was just an example that demonstrates how, in that moment and in so many others like it, I was saying "yes" to all sorts of things and people—except God. And the loudest voice I tend to listen to other than God's is my own. As a stubborn and strong-willed person, I often do and think what is right in my own eyes. My mother told me that I've been that way since I was a child. She said that I had no fear and I would go with anyone who opened their arms up to me because that was my instinct, even when she told me to stay close to her. Don't get me wrong, instincts aren't a bad thing, but doing what's right in my own eyes is, especially when it involves compromising my safety and ignoring the will of God.

At times, we've all fallen into the trap of testing God. We probably do this more often than we think. Think about it; how many times have we asked God to bless a mess? Even when that mess might be completely contrary to something He has already clearly addressed in His Word.

Have you ever asked Him to give you something that you couldn't afford? I have. I remember once I wanted a house that I couldn't afford. I did everything in my power to make it happen. I changed mortgage lenders. I took money from my savings and my retirement. I prayed and prayed and continually asked God to work it out. And, the more I prayed, the more it failed to work out. The lender saw my desperation and tried to find ways to help me figure out solutions. None of which worked out. But, still, I pushed and pushed and finally made it to closing. I thought that I was finally vindicated and was ready to put my signature on all the paperwork. But, when I started to sign, something just wasn't quite right. I looked, and there it was in writing. The rate on the note was different from the one on the deed. I thought, "How could this happen? The devil just doesn't want me to have this." So, I thought I should keep pushing, and therefore called the lender while I was at closing to determine how to fix the problem—and he hung up on me. I thought that surely it was a mistake and called him back, and he hung up again. The title company told me to just sign everything and keep my check, and we would figure everything out in the morning.

I was exhausted and began to pray a different prayer that night. I began to ask God, why was I getting so much resistance in this situation? And He answered back loud and clear with the question, why do you want this house? I was confused, because I thought, don't You want me to have good things? And He took me to Luke 14:28 . . . count the cost. In the text, Jesus is speaking to the apostles about discipleship and the types of sacrifices they would need to make to follow Him, but He was also speaking to me about the practicality of embarking on an endeavor before I sat down and considered what was involved. So, I swallowed my pride and the next day called the lender—who then proceeded at first to indicate that I could be sued because I did not follow through with my obligation to perform. This time, I sought Godly counsel and was advised not to go to closing based on their mistake. I followed this advice and was able to walk away without any further implications. In this case, in order to say "yes" to God, I had to say "no" to myself. In other words, I was intent on making it happen, with or without God's or anyone else's opinion on the matter. And when we do this, we can potentially block God's plan and what God truly has for us.

Does this resonate with you? Do you want God's best, or do you want what you want regardless?

Better yet, what about when we ask Him for something that is completely against His will and have the nerve to get mad when He doesn't answer back? Especially when we already know what His Word says on the matter. Like when we covet something that belongs to someone else, or when we wish God would move someone out of our way so that we can do what we want. The Word of God says clearly, "Beloved, let us love one another, for love is of God" (1 John 4:7a, NKJV). But we sometimes want to pick and choose who we apply that to, especially if someone thinks differently or acts independently of how we think they should.

Truth be told, I have had to repent so many times because I have feared man more than I have feared God. That includes fearing what others think of me if I don't live a certain way or have certain possessions that are a sign of someone who is doing well in my own eyes. Or, fearing that people wouldn't like me if they knew I think and act differently from them. This has happened in so many situations. Who cares, anyway? God says that He is my Shepherd and that I should fear not, because He is with me. Bye, Felicia!

In other words, there are some things that we don't even have to ask or pray about. Think about that for a moment. Do we really need to pray about asking God to harm someone else on our behalf? Do we really need to pray about using our tithe money at the casino? Do we really need to pray and ask God to take something from someone else to give to us, when He said that He owns the cattle on a thousand hills? Perhaps what we really need to ask God for is the grace and favor to deal with our current situation, and more importantly, the motive behind some of our selfish desires. And, when we can have an honest conversation with ourselves, we can sometimes uncover what God is trying to give us instead of what we think He wants to take away.

These are the things that really weigh us down, just like the moocher, who just wants more and more. More of your time. More of your energy. More of your livelihood. They take up our concentration and take our focus away from God. And He deserves so much more than what we sometimes give him. The interesting point about it all is that it's coming from you and me. Those things represent our flesh, that part of us that God is constantly trying to prune away so that the new man or woman can come forward.

Sometimes we have to give up on our own way and say "no" to ourselves. Once we do, we can move forward and move on to obtaining what God has for us. I can certainly say that I have let things that are familiar get close to me that weren't the will of God. They are the will of me, myself, and I. And those were the times where occasionally I needed to be checked. In fact, truth be told, we all do. A good illustration of this is in the game of basketball. When a player wants to make sure the other team is ready, they pass the ball to an opponent and say "check." The opposing player replies back by also saying "check." Just like in basketball, sometimes we need to let the Big Baller bounce on us and check to make sure we are in the right place.

Self-examination can be tough because there's always a chance that you might not like what you see. I would be the first one to admit that one of the hardest things that I've had to do is to put a mirror in front of my own face and take a look at what I see—and accept what it is I'm seeing. And beyond that, I've needed to learn to speak about myself in accordance with what God says about me, as opposed to what my own emotions say. That means examining motivations and influencers. After all, those are the things and people we are submitting to at any given time. And, whether we want to admit it or not, we all submit to someone or something. So, the challenge is always to be able to examine yourself and thereby find out who or what you're submitting to.

If I find myself going through a draining or stressful pattern that persists, I often have to ask myself to examine why it is repeating. Is there something that I haven't learned, or is there something I have not done that I already know to do? What am I missing? Am I submitting to God?

The whole point of the self-check is to help you identify where you are and compare it to where you want to be. Job 28:28 (KJV) cautions us, "Behold, the fear of the Lord, that is wisdom; and to depart from evil is understanding." So, why do we rely on our instincts and take it for granted that things will always work out?

By the way, a few years ago, I was attending a birthday party for a friend in the neighborhood I grew up in and saw several people that I hadn't seen in years. I had to catch myself because I couldn't always remember names or faces. I had to stare for a long time at one person in particular, a man who was wearing a suit that fit just right, because I remembered him, but couldn't recall his name. I went over to see if I could figure out why he looked so familiar, and his name came to me, but not any details. I smiled and he smiled back. I said, "Hi, Marty. How are you doing?" He fired back, "Call me Martin," and shook my hand. And once again I was caught off guard. It suddenly came to me that this was the crackhead from twenty-five years ago—and not only was he restored back to the tall, dark, and handsome dude I remembered, he was also actively rejecting his old name and his old life. He rewrote his story. Bye, Felicia!

The point that I'm trying to make is that sometimes, in order to say "yes, God," we have to say no to ourselves and to the things that mooch from what God has for us. And believe me, I want everything He has in store for me. He is unmatched in His goodness and His love is unfailing. He actually wants to give you so much more than you can think of or imagine.

Prayer is very important in helping you crucify your flesh and become aligned with God. Pray about whether your motives and influences are coming from God. If they are not, ask God to help you replace them with His will. One way you can do this is to mention the things you know are coming from your will and not God's, and say out loud, "Bye, _____," filling in your own name. You can also begin praying the scriptures, which helps us get our prayers better aligned with what God says about the matter. Some examples would be:

Lord, in Your Word You say that You would keep my mind in perfect peace if I keep my mind on You, so I ask that You would show me how to rest in You. (Isaiah 26:3)

According to Your Word, You said that no weapon formed against me would prosper, so I ask that You would help me to stand still and see the salvation of the Lord. (Isaiah 54:17)

Your Word says that by Your stripes, we are healed, so I ask that You would bring healing to my mind, body, and spirit. (Isaiah 53:5)

In Your Word, You say that if I be faithful over a few things, You would make me ruler over many, so I ask

You to show me how to be faithful and grateful for what You've given me. (Matthew 25:21)

I am not a preacher, teacher, or Bible scholar. I am a woman of God seeking after the things of God. I hope that my testimony of saying "yes" to God and "bye" to Stacy has encouraged you to move forward and to crucify your flesh, so that you can discover what it is that God has for you.

What Does Your Garden Reflect?

Michele Noel-Peake

And the Lord God planted a garden in Eden, in the east, and there he put the man whom he had formed.

GENESIS 2:8 (ESV)

OUR GARDEN

God gave me a powerful vision years ago which helped to bring clarity to my life unlike anything I had ever had before. It has helped me greatly ever since, and I would like to share that vision with you. The vision God gave me was to start to see my life as a beautiful garden. A garden He had given to me. As you read through the remainder of this chapter, I want you to think of your life as a garden God has given to you. God is the owner of the garden, but you are the caretaker, just like Adam was in the Garden of Eden. We aren't in Eden today. However, we are in the garden of our individual lives. My garden is called Michele, and your garden, your life, is called by your name.

Besides you, what's in your garden, and what do you do with it? Great question. In your garden is everything God has ever given to you to manage and care for. It's things like your health, marriage, finances, job, ministry, and, most of all, Him. Our God, as the Owner, Creator, and Master Architect of our garden, has given us a major rule that can't be ignored. The rule is that everything you do in your garden has to be done *with* God. You and I need His Spirit like a flower needs rain. Without the Spirit of God working in us, we won't be able to sustain the garden, grow the garden, nurture the garden, and protect the garden. The good news and advantage we have today is that Jesus Christ made a way for us to have the Spirit of God in us twenty-four hours a day through the Holy Spirit. We can all take a praise break right there! Thank You, Jesus! He made it possible, by His finished works on the cross and His resurrection three days later, that as long as we abide in Him and He in us, we will be able to produce much fruit in the garden of our lives.

I just love gazing at a beautifully kept garden and being in the presence of its natural beauty. When we feed ourselves with the Word of God, connect with the living water of the Holy Spirit, and praise God through our obedience, we beautify the gardens of our life.

Saying "yes, God" boils down to us caring for our gardens, our lives, and making them grow and become fruitful by His Spirit. But our gardens won't get there without hard work on our part. Any landscaper, gardener, or farmer will tell you with great certainty that gardening takes a lot of hard work. The scripture that comes to my mind is Luke 9:23 (KJV), which says, "Then He said to them all, 'If anyone desires to come after Me, let him deny himself, and take up his cross daily, and follow Me.'"

Jesus told us from the very beginning that we all would have a cross to bear, a price to pay for living the true life of a believer in Jesus Christ.

The great thing about an amazing garden is that it says a lot about its gardener. And just like we are a reflection of our God, made in His image, a beautiful garden is a reflection of its gardener. What has God given to you? What is He calling you to? And do you know His voice? These are questions I want you to ask yourself. Saying "yes, God" will be the single most important two words you and I will ever say in our entire lives. I had to face the same question God is still asking us today, and that is—What does your garden reflect? A "yes, God" or a "no, God"?

BARRIERS TO YES, GOD

Saying "yes, God" comes with so much power that our enemy is still trying to block it like he did in the garden with Adam and Eve. The only difference is that he is not a snake anymore. This enemy is fighting us in the invisible, spiritual realm today in many ways.

This real enemy knows the power a "yes, God" can have to change our entire life around for the better. Our enemy is still lurking around, trying to get into our gardens. He wants to stop us from getting what God has for us on the other side of our "yes, God." His main plan is to kill, steal, and destroy our "yes" to God. And if we are not careful, he will get into our garden and create weeds to choke out the life and beauty of what God is trying to do in and through us.

Today, our enemy still uses doubt, deception, division, the pride of life, selfishness, conceit, and all kinds of sins to keep you and me from the Truth. It is so important to be mindful of his tactics. The enemy of our life truly has no power unless we give it to him. And one of the ways we give him permission to mess around in our lives is by telling God "no" or simply ignoring Him when He is trying to get our attention. Remember that major rule, that without God, we are powerless against our enemies, which include the devil, our flesh, which can be our biggest enemy, and the world.

A "yes, God" is powerful, but it can be painful at the same time. Our natural inclination is to avoid pain. And sometimes, to protect ourselves from feeling it at all, we will begin to put up a wall, our own barriers. As a result, while it keeps the pain caused by others out, it also keeps God out. The only solution, when we feel pain or fear of any kind, is to simply say . . . "yes, God" and trust Him. When I felt the pain of losing six pregnancies, I had to say yes, God, you can comfort me.

As God is calling on us to fulfill the purpose He has for us on this earth, we have to surrender and submit ourselves fully to Him and let down the barriers we have built. I had to make a decision years ago to say yes, God, I will let you protect me. I will stop trying to protect myself when I feel attacked by others. That simple prayer brought down a barrier in my life. Immediately, I felt free, I felt that I did not have to fight those battles anymore; I could surrender them to God. Ask God to show you the barriers you have up that are blocking Him in this season of your life.

THE COST

Saying "yes" to God will always cost us something—but I want you to shift your thinking. No longer see it as what it will *cost you*. Look at it from the position of what it already *cost Him*. Your *yes* and my *yes* will never cost us as much as it did Jesus, because it cost Him His life. He actually paid the ultimate price for you and me. In fact, it's because of Him we even have the privilege of saying *yes, God*!

Jesus laid down His life for you and me when we were yet still sinners, and that says a lot about His true love for us. He didn't have to lay down His life. He simply "wanted" to so that you and I might be saved and have an abundant life *in* Him.

Do you remember how Jesus asked God to take this cup from Him? Where was Jesus, then? In a garden on assignment for God, just like you and I are on assignment for God. Jesus said to the Father, "nevertheless, Your will be done." That was Jesus saying "yes, God." Our God the Father needed a human sacrifice to fix what Adam had done in the garden. His sin when he and Eve ate the apple separated us from God. The human sacrifice was God's very own Son, Jesus the Christ. And no one could ever pay what Jesus paid for us on the cross, nor what He did for us when He got up on that third day! So let's take another look at our lives. Is God asking us to get on a physical cross? Nope! Jesus did that already. He's simply asking for you and me to be obedient to His Word so that our gardens may reflect a "yes, God," just like Jesus. Let's look at a few things *yes, God* can cost us . . .

When we say "yes" to God, we are also saying "no" to our will. The moment I say "yes" to God is also the same moment that I say "no" to Michele. In our will, we want what we want. And we can sometimes be selfish and prideful, thinking only about fulfilling our fleshly desires. But when we say "yes, God," we are really saying to God, "I surrender my thoughts and my ways to Yours."

When we say "yes" to God, we will lose some things and some people. Not everyone or everything will be able to come with us when God is calling us to something new. We have to be willing to accept those losses and say "yes, God" anyway. Some people are only in our life for a season.

When we say "yes" to God, we are saying "bye" to our comfort and our feelings. A few years back, God showed me that it was time for me to get comfortable with being uncomfortable. It's not natural for us to want to be uncomfortable, and I was no exception, but it's the only way to walk in faith and truly trust God. Being willing to be naked and vulnerable when we say "yes, God" is a critical part of the process, and I had to experience it in spite of my feeling scared, lonely, confused, and perhaps even angry or hurt at times. I am still learning to surrender my comfort to God. In these vulnerable moments, I had to learn to put on my spiritual clothes of humility, prayer, and praising God through it all!

OUR SACRIFICE

Not only is there a cost to saying "yes God," there is also a sacrifice to saying "yes, God." Jesus already made the ultimate sacrifice on our behalf. So when I think of a sacrifice on our part, I think of Romans 12:1–2 (NKJV): "I beseech you therefore, brethren, by the mercies of God, that you present your bodies a living sacrifice, holy, acceptable to God, which is your reasonable service. And do not be conformed to this world, but be transformed by the renewing of your mind, that you may prove what is that good and acceptable and perfect will of God."

Saying "yes, God" means that you and I are sacrificing ourselves. Our old habits and customs must die. And we have to kill them by the renewing of our minds daily, based on the Word of God. There is no way to be a great gardener or landscaper without studying and learning about what it takes to nurture, plant, water, and care for your garden. The main thing we want to study is the

Creator of the garden. Studying the Creator gives us insight about ourselves. After all, remember we are made in His image. Neglecting to intentionally read and study the Word of God means neglecting the understanding of who we truly are! That's where we gain the knowledge and spiritual strength to say "yes, God!"

Giving God our everything (sleep, eating, work, relationships, spouses, children, spiritual walk, etc.) is the very least that we can do for all that He has done for us! It took me meditating on this scripture for two years before I truly understood it, and it's still a battle!

THE BEAUTIFUL BLESSINGS

I can most assuredly tell you that the costs and the sacrifice are so worth all of the blessings in saying "yes, God!" I simply cannot count the endless blessings I have received as a result of saying "yes, God!" And it's not just me, because God is no respecter of persons. I know so many people who have said "yes, God," and the windows of heaven have opened up for them, too!

There have been so many times when I have said "yes, God," including forgiving those who have hurt me, mistreated me, disappointed me, and even lied to me. And there have also been plenty of times in my life when I have not said "yes" to God, and it has cost me such unnecessary hurt, pain, and disappointment that, as I grow in Him, I seek to make those times few in number.

My greatest "yes, God" moment by far was receiving His Son, Jesus Christ, as my Lord and Savior. It's the permanent security of knowing beyond a shadow of a doubt that I am one day going to spend eternity with my Father in heaven. This truth is unrivaled. The sweetest part is the promise we have. The promise of experiencing heaven on Earth with the Holy Spirit inside of us. Just leading and guiding us until we are called home by our Father.

"Yes, God" will not always be easy, but it certainly will be worth every single ounce of blessings it comes with. The fact that God is calling us to Himself to be used for His good purpose is an enormous blessing in and of itself. It says that God is not finished with us. There is more work He has for us to accomplish in our gardens while here on Earth.

Yes, I've lost houses, cars, and money, I've experienced health issues and challenges, I have had numerous miscarriages, family drama, disappointments, and a whole lot more. I would absolutely do it all over again to have this intense, indescribable, incredible relationship with Jesus Christ! Plus, there are so many perks that come with this relationship. Perks like joy, peace, fulfillment, purpose, and the best relationship in the whole entire world! It wasn't always the case, but those eternal things mean so much more to me than the material things of the world. These blessings are irreplaceable. And once you get a taste of them, you will never want to let the blessings go again. The only access to these blessings is through our "yes, God!" There is no other way, no matter how hard we try!

I used to think I needed certain things from family members, like validation and approval. And if I did not get it, I felt inadequate and undervalued. But, as my relationship has grown with God and my "yes, God" moments have grown in number, I no longer feel that way. I know my value is wrapped up in my "yes, God." Yes, God, I believe every word You say about me. Yes, God, You created me uniquely and fearfully and wonderfully! You gave me freedom and the kind of love and validation that no one can take away from me because the world did not give it to me.

I have also come to realize that as God was emptying out of me the mess that was in me, He was also filling me back up with messages of His goodness to share with others! God could not use my pride and self-righteousness in my garden. I started to notice that, as pride and self-righteousness took a backseat in my life, humility was able to step forward. With humility came a much closer relationship with God. As this relationship with God grew, so did my love and my faith! What does God still need to empty out of you?

As I read God's Word, studied His Word, meditated on His Word, and spent time with Him, time in prayer and throughout my day, I noticed that I became more comfortable with surrendering to the Holy Spirit's prompting and hearing God's still, small, quiet voice directing me on caring for my garden. God also placed people around me to show me the way. I'm grateful for the provisions He put in place for the times I may have missed Him. Having an encouraging church family and spiritual leaders are also extremely valuable blessings from God.

The fruit produced in my garden now, as a result of saying "yes, God," has been an enormous blessing to me . . . if I could say "yes," you can too.

It was saying "yes, God" to preaching His Word that birthed sermons which have impacted many lives.

It was saying "yes, God" to getting rid of a toxic relationship that made my relationship with God stronger.

Saying "yes, God" to handing in my resignation made more room for walking in my real, true purpose and calling.

Saying "yes, God" to starting and serving in ministries at my church produced many opportunities to help others and to lift up God's kingdom, all at the same time.

THE BIGGEST YES!

Above all of the "yes, God" moments in your life, the one with the greatest impact and power is the "yes, God" for eternal security in heaven. When your days are up on Earth, you want to know there is a place prepared for you already in heaven. No other "yes, God" moment will ever be as significant as this one. In fact, all of our opportunities to say "yes, God" are rooted in our salvation. So I plead with you on behalf of heaven that, if you are not saved and have not said "yes, God" in the area of your eternal security, your salvation, this would be your starting point. Please say "yes, God" to accept His Son, Jesus Christ, as your Lord and Savior and to receive the Holy Spirit.

If you feel the slightest nudge or inkling down on the inside of you that God may be calling you into His Kingdom, say "yes, God" today! If you desire to be a part of the divine work God is doing here on Earth and you want to have an eternal home to go to in heaven when you pass from this earth, say "yes, God" today! This "yes, God" prayer is a matter of life and death. But you must believe it in your heart first that Jesus is who He says that He is. Believe that He can do what He says He can do. Go ahead and confess with your mouth through prayer that Jesus is the Son of God and that He died for your sins. And ask for His forgiveness, being willing in your heart to turn away from your sins and turn to His righteousness. Finally, let Him know that you make Him Lord of your life! If you have said this prayer, accepting Jesus as Lord and confessing your sins, and you believe it and are willing to repent, find a local Bible-based church. Find a place where you can grow, be encouraged by other believers, and receive strength in your walk with Jesus. Find a place where you discover and use your spiritual gifts to uplift His Kingdom. Congratulations on your salvation; God bless you, and welcome to the Kingdom of God! You now have the power to live a life of freedom with

God! There is no other name by which we have access to God, except through Jesus Christ! As it says in Acts 4:12 (ESV), "And there is salvation in no one else, for there is no other name under heaven given among men by which we must be saved." Now get ready, get ready, get ready!

YOU CAN DO THIS!

For you and I who truly love Him and are called by Him, I say this—If God is calling you to say "yes" to a ministry, go ahead and tell Him "yes." If He is asking you to pick up the phone and forgive someone who hurt or offended you, go ahead and say "yes." If He called you to teach, teach! Preach, preach! Move, move! Start a business, start a business! And only you know the areas that need focus in your life. What is God calling you to say "yes" to?

My brothers and sisters, there is no greater life to live than a life that is surrendered to the One who created us! No longer put off your "yes, God." You have been putting it off long enough. With the times we are living in today, God wants all of His children to be better prepared for what He has next in our life. You and I won't find true peace unless we say "yes, God."

Yes it will cost you, yes it will mean sacrificing yourself, yes it will mean surrendering your will, but the blessings on the other side will be more than worth it! So what are you waiting for? Let your garden reflect God today. Tell Him . . . *Yes, God*!

Sources

About the Authors

Ashley McNeill, twenty-five, is the founder of Elevate Ya-self, LLC, an international crisis manager, a Jesus-loving Christian, a public speaker, and a disaster relief specialist, and is certified in nonprofit management. Ashley is the recipient of the Global Citizen award from Gettysburg College, where she obtained a BA in political science. Throughout her lifetime of travelling and volunteering in underprivileged communities around the world, she has become conscious of the disparity of resources specifical-ly between developed and developing countries. Ashley has dedicated her life to serving others by assisting phys-ically through the distribution of resources overseas. She is led by Philippians 2:4 (ERV): "Don't be interested only in your own life, but care about the lives of others too." Within her business, Elevate Yaself, Ashley does philan-thropic coaching to empower and guide individuals to use their God-given talents to pursue passion projects, open businesses, and create social impact.

Learn more at www.ashleymcneill.com

Crystal M. Adair is an author, playwright, speaker, teacher, and Washington, DC, native. She graduated from Clark Atlanta University with a degree in mass media arts (radio-television-film). For the past twenty years, Crystal has taught English, public speaking, and theater to K–12 and college students in California, Maryland, and the nation's capitol. In 2017, she self-published her titular testimony, *Therapy: A Memoir Novella by Crystal M. Adair*. This work chronicles Crystal's harrowing journey of abandonment, adoption, abuse, grief, and depression, but it also details her "But God" breakthrough and transformational healing. Crystal now inspires and empowers others with her message, hoping someday to have her own speaking tour. She has also written and directed more than forty stage plays about social justice, humanitarian causes, and African American culture. Crystal currently resides in Prince George's County, Maryland, with her smart, musical, and wonderfully witty teenage son, Jalen Christopher.

Learn more at www.crystaladair.com

Catherine Jones is originally from Harrisburg, Pennsylvania, but has been a Maryland resident for the last fifteen years. She received her bachelor's degree in marketing from IUP and has excelled in her career as a senior pharmaceutical sales representative for leading global pharmaceutical companies such as Eli Lilly.

Catherine is the founder and senior pastor of House of Myriad Ministries, and is a daughter of Mount Calvary Baptist Church under Senior Pastor Charles E. Cato, Sr. She is also a student at Maple Springs Baptist Bible College and Seminary, pursuing a master of arts degree in divinity.

Minister Catherine is very active in church ministry, doing missionary work and preaching overseas to spread the Gospel of Jesus Christ in Africa, Guyana, and Trinidad. She has also traveled to Israel to walk in the footsteps of Jesus, which has given her a heightened passion for discipleship.

To connect, email her at Houseofmyriad@gmail.com

Inga Robinson answered her call to ministry and was ordained as a deacon in 2001. She worked in various positions within the finance and banking industry and is presently employed by Georgetown University Law Center in Washington, DC. Her motivational gifts and talents have resulted in opportunities to preach, teach, and facilitate workshops across the USA and abroad.

Inga works with religious, civic, and nonprofit organizations to serve residents in the inner city of the Washington, DC, metropolitan area and as an overseas missionary. As the director of summer programs with Training Grounds Inc., located in Washington, DC, and in partnership with First Lady Michelle Obama's public health and healthy lifestyle campaign Let's Move, she worked to provide nutritious meals to the underserved populations in the community.

Deacon Inga birthed a powerful ministry for teen girls called "Ladies Of Virtuous Etiquette" (L.O.V.E. Ministry), which innovatively ministers to teen girls about *real life* issues.

To connect, email her at ingarobinson2011@yahoo.com

Tammeca Riley, MS, is a certified professional résumé writer with a specialized certification in writing résumés for military-to-civilian transitions. She helps professionals and military veterans and retirees by writing creative career marketing résumés, content for LinkedIn profiles, and cover letters to facilitate pursuit of various career paths in the federal government and private sector. Tammeca's résumé writing work is featured in *Expert Resumes for Managers and Executives (4th edition)*.

Tammeca is a member of the Professional Association of Résumé Writers & Career Coaches (PARW/CC), where she serves as a certification committee member. She is also a member of Career Directors International (CDI) and Career Thought Leaders (CTL). Formerly, Tammeca served as a youth leadership program co-coordinator, area director, and member of Toastmasters International, an educational organization that teaches public speaking and leadership skills.

Tammeca and her husband have four children.

Learn more at linkedin.com/in/TammecaRiley

Stacy Bradner is a program manager at the University of Maryland Global Campus in Largo, Maryland, and is currently pursuing her passion for health and wellness. Stacy loves people and strives to find the best in herself and others. She believes that we should take care of our whole selves . . . body, mind, and spirit. She values reconciliation and unity. Her future goals include opening a bed and breakfast in the metropolitan area where people will be able to find peace, energy, and a renewed spirit. She believes that with God, all things are possible.

Stacy has an MBA from the University of Maryland Global Campus and a master's degree in communications from Howard University. She also has several business certifications, including a PMP and SHRM-SCP. She belongs to several church and community organizations that promote health, the arts, and making one's own community a better place.

To connect, email her at stacybradner@verizon.net

Michele Noel-Peake is always humbled when God uses her to impact lives. Whether through her preaching a message, teaching a class, facilitating a workshop, or coaching a client, she is passionate about using her gifts, talents, and skills to help empower and elevate others.

Michele is a two-time Amazon bestselling author with several awards for her public speaking. She has been acknowledged for her advocacy work in the community with domestic violence and is grateful for the opportunity to speak to thousands internationally.

With a BS in business, Michele has held many leadership positions in corporate America and serves in several ministries at Mount Calvary Baptist Church, where she was licensed to preach by her spiritual father, Pastor Charles E. Cato, Sr.

She started Michele Renee Consulting to better serve both her personal and professional clients and the greater community through her life-changing coaching, facilitation, and training services.

Learn more at www.michelereneeconsulting.com

To inquire or book coaching, facilitation
or speaking engagements,
please contact Michele at

www.michelereneeconsulting.com
on Facebook @ Michele Renee Consulting
and on YouTube @ Michele Renee Consulting

COACHING TRAINING FACILITATION
MICHELE RENEE CONSULTING

purposely created
PUBLISHING

CREATING DISTINCTIVE BOOKS
WITH INTENTIONAL RESULTS

We're a collaborative group of creative masterminds
with a mission to produce high-quality books to position
you for monumental success in the marketplace.

Our professional team of writers, editors, designers,
and marketing strategists work closely together to ensure
that every detail of your book is a clear representation
of the message in your writing.

Want to know more?
Write to us at info@publishyourgift.com
or call (888) 949-6228

Discover great books, exclusive offers, and more at
www.PublishYourGift.com

Connect with us on social media

@publishyourgift